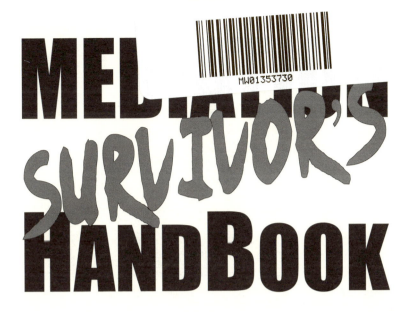

Peg Nichols

Thos. Britt Nichols, JD, Editor

WEIR BOX PUBLISHING

WEIR BOX PUBLISHING
OLATHE, KANSAS
www.mediationsurvivorshandbook.com

Copyright © 2006 Margaret Y. Nichols
All rights reserved under International and Pan-American Copyright Conventions.

No part of this book may be reproduced or transmitted in any form or by any means electronic, mechanical or physical including photocopying, recording or by any information storage or retrieval system, without permission in writing from the author.

Published in the United States by Weir Box Publishing of Olathe, Kansas.

Library of Congress Control Number: 2006930298

Publisher's Cataloging-in-Publication Data

Nichols, Peg
    Mediation Survivor's HandBook / Peg Nichols; [edited by] Thos. Britt Nichols, JD
    p. cm.
    1st ed.
    ISBN 0-9778711-0-X

1. Mediation. 2. Conflict management. 3. Dispute resolution (Law). 4. Family mediation. 5. Peer counseling of students 6. Restorative justice. 7. Family mediation. 8. Mediation--Vocational guidance. I. Title.

K2390 .N53 2006
347.09--dc22   2006930298

This work is dedicated to

GARY L SHANK
Panel: 01W   Line: 59

TABLE OF CONTENTS

Introducing the Author vii

Chapter One
It's All About Survival 1
(Take Charge of Your Life ... Or Someone Else Might)

Chapter Two
Nuts and Bolts 6
(Things You Need to Know—and Understand)

Chapter Three
Your Better Judgment 35
(Getting Started)

Chapter Four
Controlling the Split. 49
(Mediation in Divorce)

Chapter Five
Healing the Hurt. 57
(Mediation after Crime: Finding Solace)

Chapter Six
Them Ain't No Small Potatoes 67
(Mediation not Litigation)

Chapter Seven
School Yard Games 78
(Mediation and Our Kids)

Chapter Eight
Getting Your Share. 82
(Probate Mediation)

Chapter Nine
Who Invented Mediation? 86
(Does it Matter?)

Chapter Ten
Why Not You?. 93
(Exploring Mediation and You)

Chapter Eleven
GUIDEPOSTS. 101
(Making Mediation Work for YOU)

ACKNOWLEDGEMENTS 108
To Everyone Who Has Shared My Journey

The Art of the Book 110

Portland, Oregon
January, 2006

It is only fitting that a young mother whose favorite method of solving squabbles between her sons (her daughter almost always remained above the fray) centered on the admonition—"If you can't work things out between yourselves, then I may have to do it for you!"—should grow up to become a mediator and come to write a book about mediation.

That the same young mother would later come to see mediation as a valuable tool for peace and dispute resolution is also not a surprise. That young mother, your author and my mother, grew to adulthood in an astonishing age of previously unimagined military power rivaled only by the astonishing amount of its use and effectiveness that has been exhibited in our daily lives through modern communications. No one need look far to see evidence of what happens when disputes cannot be resolved with civility and dignity. Her personal application of "think global, act local," your author believes that if mediation can be used to solve conflicts between nations, and it can, and if mediation can be used to solve conflicts between individuals or groups, and it can, then someone needs to use it. And she has. In her life and in others.

As a twice-retired (from a career as a foreign language teacher in public schools and later as a newspaper publisher) but never-too-tired sexagenarian, she spent a decade serving her County's small claims court, first as a volunteer and later as program coordinator, helping to establish and organize mediation as an alternative to trial. When that proved not to be enough to keep her pinned down, she traveled to other countries, including war-torn Guatemala, drug-torn Colombia and religiously-torn North Ireland in low-key but high-risk peace efforts to help plant seeds of mediation as a potential path to peace—locally, neighbor to neighbor, and then globally, neighbor to neighbor. Her guiding thought has been to demonstrate the values of mediation through small efforts with hopes that the example might rub off on the bigger issues. Someone has to set an example. She seems to think that training mediators—and mediation—is a good place to start.

I was working in my law office one day. It hadn't been a particularly good day or bad day of lawyering. There had been an average number of appearances before the judges and an average number of conferences with other lawyers and an average amount of pain, discourse, acrimony and advocacy. Your author called me, which was rare enough, and after a few minutes of small talk, rarer still, she blurted out: "I hate lawyers!" I didn't want to ask: "All lawyers?" I wasn't certain I wanted to know her answer. I asked her, instead, whether she thought that after 25 years of being one I liked lawyers any better.

I don't believe that she hates all lawyers. In fact, I know she doesn't hate any person—lawyer or otherwise. What I think she hates—and she would not be alone in this by any stretch of the imagination—is the way that our lawyer-dense legal system sometimes seems to put expensive and time consuming barriers between people. I know that she understands that the rules in place and the roles that lawyers play in our legal system are there for a purpose—that some disputes can't be resolved without full application of courts and processes and appeals ad plentium. But it is difficult for her to stand by and watch small problems made big by one-size-fits-all rules in what she calls the "big dog courts." I hope that she also understands that wise lawyers, the kind her son continues to aspire to be, know that mediation is an excellent tool with a broad range of application to both large and small disputes that offers economies of money, time, resources and emotions while empowering the participants to find their own meaningful and acceptable solutions to life's disputations. Those same wise lawyers also know that mediation can repair and even strengthen the all-too-infrequent and all-too-fragile human connections in our world.

That said, I hope that you enjoy my mother's thoughts on mediation from the participant's point of view written, as it was, out of a score or more of years of experience with mediation and a love for the goodness that can be found in people when they are given the chance.

Britt Nichols

IT'S ALL ABOUT SURVIVAL
(Take Charge of Your Life ...
... Or Someone Else Might)

Chapter One

Maybe you first heard the word **mediation** from the lips of a judge and you thought s/he was talking about someone else, not you.

Or you heard some television coverage about a **mediator** being sent to a war-torn part of the world and you thought it would be a good idea if those folks would just calm down and let some mediator tell them how to bring an end to the conflict.

Perhaps your neighbor griped for years about your cottonwood tree. Now, you're hearing from other neighbors that the complainer wants to try some of that mediation stuff on you. You are worried or offended that someone doesn't like you—or your tree.

Maybe the shop that bought some materials from your company believes that you delivered shoddy goods, or somehow double-billed them, but their manager is willing to go to mediation in order to save the trouble and expense of a lawsuit and to try to preserve the business relationship.

Is the problem that your ex-spouse—or soon-to-be ex-spouse—is being unreasonable about the kids, or visitation, or support? And your attorney is muttering that you both belong in mediation?

Or maybe you've already been to divorce court, and

> Because **mediation** comes to mean what the parties define it to be, there is no single exacting definition of "mediation." However, a good working definition is: "a process in which a mediator assists and facilitates two or more parties to a controversy in reaching a mutually acceptable resolution of the controversy and includes all contacts between a mediator and any party or agent of a party, until such time as a resolution is agreed to by the parties or the mediation process is terminated."
>
> The **mediator** is the person, trained or otherwise, accepted by all parties who conducts the mediation.

It's All About Survival

it's the judge who is ordering both parties to spend a minimum of two hours in mediation to "solve problems."

When the threat of mediation gets close to home, don't panic!

YOU CAN SURVIVE!

Not only can you survive, you can take control. In fact, to survive, you must take control—at least over your part of the mediation.

When you take control, you can come out of mediation with your dignity and self-esteem intact.

Mediation is not a threat; mediation is an opportunity.

And in the long run, you'll have some new tools you can use to tackle some of life's vexing—or not so tiny—problems. Mediation is an opportunity to use your new tools to find a **resolution** to the **dispute**.

> **Dispute** means whatever it is that the parties aren't able to agree about. It covers a wide range of things. The disagreement might be big. Or it might seem small. There may be one issue or many. But every concern is meaningful to one party or the other. It may be that one party can't even understand what the big deal is in the first place. In fact, that kind of misunderstanding—an unwillingness or inability to understand the other person's concerns—might be the basis of the entire disagreement. Whatever the cause, the disagreement is called the dispute. Another word for dispute is conflict. You may hear people talk about mediation as conflict resolution. It can be—if you learn how to use it.

If you are asked to participate in mediation, seize the opportunity. In mediation you do not have to remain silent while someone else makes decisions regarding your family, your work, your money, and your life. The beauty—the very purpose—of mediation is that the decisions—even the decision to decide—are yours.

Don't be misinformed—or even worse, intimidated—when confronted with mediation.

> **Resolution** means a dispute-ending agreement willingly entered into by the parties that resolves some or all of the parties' issues and concerns. Anything less than completely voluntary by all of the parties is not a resolution. The resolution is called a Mediation Agreement. The wisdom of a written Mediation Agreement upon the resolution of the dispute is discussed in Chapter Three.

As the rest of this book will show you, learning about mediation can empower you to take an active role, to speak your mind, to offer creative solutions to whatever dispute is being mediated. Remember: it is your dispute—it is your mediation. Mediation gives you the right, and the power, to make it your resolution. The power of self-determination to agree—or not—to a resolution of your disputes gives you control over the outcome of your dispute. The basic ideas are very simple, but very powerful. Inform yourself and …

YOU WILL SURVIVE!

IT'S ALL ABOUT SURVIVAL

ROADMAP—

Chapter Two—Nuts and Bolts: Take a quick look through Chapter Two. It may be long but it is full of essential information. You can read it now or you can always come back to it later. Browse through the other chapters and choose examples that best fit your personal situation—then come back to read Chapter Two.

NUTS AND BOLTS
*(Things You Need to Know —
and Understand)*

Chapter Two

This is the chapter you can skim—the first time through. But you will want to come back to read it more thoroughly later. It sets out the nuts and bolts of mediation.

I won't lie. This chapter contains pretty serious stuff but it will stay right here and you can come back to it later. As many times as you need.

NUTS AND BOLTS

This chapter will provide information about:

Self-Determination

Mediator Impartiality

Conflicts of Interest

Mediator Competence

Confidentiality

Quality of the Process

Advertising and Solicitations

Fees and Payments

> **ROADMAP—**
>
> You can read straight through these sections, but you should also feel free to jump right into the chapter ahead that deals with the sort of dispute you are facing. But don't forget to come back and read up on these basics.

No matter where you live, there is a core of central beliefs about mediation, what it means and how to go about it.

However, most mediators, in all honesty, will admit to the lack of a precise definition of mediation and to general confusion about some of the finer points of mediation. It is reassuring to know that amongst mediators there is remarkable similarity regarding the ethics of mediation.

Key Concepts:

Self-Determination

The starting point, no doubt about it, is self-determination. A big word, but what does it mean?

Self-determination means that if you do not agree, there is no agreement. Period. It means you cannot be forced to accept something you do not agree to accept. Your power of self-determination covers not only the subject and outcome of the mediation but also the very mediation process. If your "agreement" is not **voluntary**, it isn't an agreement.

> **Self-determination** means that if you do not willingly agree, there is no agreement. Because all parties have the same rights of self-determination, each of the parties has an equal amount of control or say over the outcome of the mediation. To reach a Mediation Agreement, all of the parties have to voluntarily agree. No one can be forced to agree by either the other parties or by a judge or the mediator.

At the same time, self-determination also means that the other party has an equal right to their own self-determination. For example, you may have an excellent suggestion about how to reach a resolution of the dispute, but if the other party does not voluntarily agree, there will not be an agreement. Self-determination makes you both powerful—but equal.

Nuts and Bolts

Neither party can make the other party agree to anything.

As you can imagine, there are many points that come up in mediation. You might decide that it is important for you to "win" on every point that comes up. Or, you might decide that it is in your best interest to yield on some things so you can gain on others (something that lots of people call "compromise"), but those decisions will always be entirely yours.

Your power—even right—of self-determination is what makes mediation different from other methods of **dispute resolution**.

The mediator is not like a judge. The mediator does not have the power to issue enforceable orders about either the process or results of mediation. The mediator cannot tell you what to do

> **Civil dispute resolution** generally consists of three different types of processes—of which **mediation** is one.
>
> The other two are the **civil courts** where judges and juries, with the help of lawyers, make decisions for you in hearings and trials, and **arbitration** where the arbitrator(s), sometimes with and sometimes without lawyers, make the rules about the process and also make decisions for you about the outcome.

and cannot decide what the outcome of the mediation will be. A judge almost always has that power. Even an arbitrator has some of those powers.

In big dog court (frequented by lawyers like Perry Mason and Johnny Cochran), it is the judge who makes the decisions. Not so in mediation. The mediator controls the mediator's role in the mediation process, but the parties have total control over the outcome. There may be no agreement at the end of a mediation session, but the parties will have made even that determination for themselves. Yes, the parties can even decide not to decide. The key to mediation is "agreement." You might be directed to mediate but you cannot be directed or ordered to "agree." That factor—your power over your decision to agree—or not—is what gives you control. It is like having your own, personal "veto" power—an uncontrolled, unlimited power to say *"No, that is not what I want to agree to."* It is what gives you self-determination.

> **Voluntary** means "of your own free will". That is, your free-will decision. It means not being forced or coerced into a resolution by anyone—including a judge. If you are being forced or required to do something by another person, it is not voluntary. At the same time, agreeing to a tempting offer as a resolution or compromising "to get it over with" is voluntary. The key is: don't agree unless—and until—you want to agree.

Closing a mediation session without a concluding Mediation Agreement does not necessarily mean failure. Mediation is invariably an educational process. At the close, even without a concluding agreement, you will know more about the feelings and motivations of the other party. You will also know more about yourself. And even without an agreement, all parties will leave with some ideas about which decisions might work best in the future so you can try to avoid the problems of the past.

People often confuse mediation with arbitration.

Don't. Mediation and arbitration are quite different—even opposites in critical ways. In arbitration another person, sometimes a panel of other persons, decides the outcome of the dispute. You might recognize the root of the word "arbitrary" in arbitration. Because you are not in control of your own decisions, arbitration can, sometimes, seem arbitrary. Many kinds of disputes are the subject of arbitration. You might agree to participate in arbitration, or you might be ordered by a judge to participate in arbitration. Some state legislatures and even Congress have passed laws requiring you to submit some disputes to arbitration. Either way, in arbitration, the ultimate decision is out of your hands—the arbitrator is there to decide the issues and the dispute. Mediation, on the other hand, gives you the power of self-determination—the power to agree or not agree to any proposed resolution.

The most important idea that you should take with you from reading this book is that, in mediation, you have the right and power of self-determination. In mediation, you—and the other party—are the persons in charge of making the decisions.

Mediator Impartiality

Mediators are only human, but good mediators will make a superhuman effort to conduct the mediation with impartiality.

In all contacts with each party, the goals of every sincere mediator will be to: treat each party equally; maintain civility and balance; and listen as attentively to one party as to the other.

If one party seems to dominate the session with a long description of her/his view of the dispute, the mediator will try to assure the silent party that her/his presence is not being overlooked, and that s/he is entitled to equal time.

Seeking impartiality, mediators worry about all sorts of things.

They spend a lot of time pondering the arrangement of the room, and where the parties sit in relationship to each other and to the mediator. For example, some mediators do not want to sit at the head of a table because it suggests that the mediator has a position of authority—even though they have absolutely no intention of issuing any orders. (And no power to issue orders either.) Good mediators dread even more being forced to sit at the same side of the table as one of the parties. The other party may too readily perceive the arrangement as an "it's me against them" situation. Round tables, or even the unbelievably rare triangle shape, make the best mediation tables. Some mediators choose to make do without a table altogether rather than to accept negative table seating. Chairs pulled up in a circle can be just fine for mediation.

In domestic or family mediations, gender balance can be a potential problem. If the circumstances allow co-mediators, the ideal combination would be one mediator of each sex.

Good mediators also fret about "small talk"—those casual remarks we all make in idle, unguarded moments. Some mediators are so cautious they will say nothing to either party unless the remark has a direct connection with the disputed matter. Do not mistake a mediator's silence for disinterest or boredom.

Yet friendly conversation is what lets us establish those human connections and helps set the tone for a relaxed atmosphere in which conflicting parties can feel comfortable in offering and exploring options for resolution.

Mediators who feel at ease with small talk will take care to keep their remarks inclusive of all parties.

How your mediation will proceed will often depend upon the individual mediator's preferences and styles. Some mediators like to have a separate meeting with each party in advance of the scheduled mediation.

Which party the mediator talks with first is usually a matter of which party is available first. Sometimes the party who is the second to be heard fears that the mediator already will be prejudiced in favor of the other party. Put that notion out of your mind—listening with an open mind is one of the mediator's most important skills. Remember, the mediator isn't "deciding" about your dispute—your power of self-determination means that you are—if you will be—in charge.

Sometimes mediators do not want to meet either party until the mediation session begins, when they can meet all parties for the first time together.

Sometimes, when the issues are complex or when setting the mediation schedule is complicated, mediators request a short written description of the dispute and the parties' positions as a way of becoming familiar with the dispute before the first meeting.

Emotions during mediations can become very intense. Mediators are quite likely to call a temporary halt to face-to-face mediation. They may say it is time for a **caucus,** a somewhat formal word mediators use because they can't come up with anything better. Some call the caucus "taking a time-out" but time-out sounds either too formal—or like someone might be in trouble! During caucus, the parties will be separated and the mediator will use the opportunity to speak first with one party, and then the other, for an approximately equal period of time.

> **Caucus** means a pause in mediation when the parties separate, sometimes to individual rooms or areas. The parties should use caucus to consider proposed resolutions or other developments. Often the mediator will visit separately with the parties during caucus. Caucus can be an appropriate time for parties to visit with any advisors. If lawyers or other advisors are part of the mediation process, caucus provides an appropriate time for them to advise their respective clients. Sometimes, a mediator might suggest taking a **recess,** sort of like an extended caucus, for a few hours, days or even a week to provide parties additional time to consider their positions or to evaluate proposals that have been left on the table.

Sometimes folks just need a break—the human body was not meant to remain forever glued to the seat of a chair. Caucus is a chance to get a drink of water, stretch your legs, and maybe go down the hall to the vending machines, if available. If you need a caucus, for any reason—or even for no reason—don't hesitate to ask for one.

Nuts and Bolts

Mediators in private practice have more lee-way in how and when the mediation and any separate meetings will be scheduled. Mediators in court-connected programs will follow court guidelines.

If any party in mediation feels the mediator is not acting impartially, s/he should feel free to confront the mediator directly, in either joint session or privately. Remember: Self-determination! But also remember, no one can know what you want unless you speak up. Along with your right and power of self-determination comes your obligation to responsibly let the mediator and other parties know what is important to you. Do not be afraid to speak up—reasonably and responsibly.

> **ROADMAP—**
>
> Are you feeling bogged down? These explanations can be tedious. Go ahead and take a leap to one of the chapters that describes your situation and then come back for these Nuts and Bolts!

Conflicts of Interest

A mediator should never try to resolve a dispute in which s/he has any interest in the outcome. A mediator cannot be on either "side."

Avoiding conflicts of interest can be a little tricky.

Many mediators are so conscious of preserving impartiality they do not want to know anything about either party until they are able to meet the parties together at the same time—often for the first time.

And yet mediators do need some basic information so they don't unexpectedly find themselves being asked to mediate with their brother-in-law's boss, the mother of their child's best friend, or someone against whom they are competing for business. Many community mediation centers and small claims dispute resolution programs are served by volunteer mediators, all of whom are engaged in all sorts of other activities, both business and personal in and about your community.

Minor conflicts can be bridged, if they are fully acknowledged. Any potential conflict of interest should be openly discussed, perhaps even with each party separately. This problem is a slippery slope, however, and the mediation should continue only if all parties are comfortable with the circumstances of the conflict of interest after full and open discussion.

Concerns about conflicts of interest can lead to questions about using an **inside mediator** or an **outside mediator.** Will the mediation process be better served if the mediator already possesses significant knowledge about the subject of the debate? Or are the issues more carefully defined and potential resolutions more clearly expressed if the mediator's lack of knowledge encourages greater openness in examining the circumstances?

Conflicts of interest may be more likely to arise in commercial, small claims, or civil mediation than in domestic or family mediation. A mediator in a community mediation center, for example, may be very well informed about technical aspects of making a wise selection of paint products and applying them properly because s/he owns a paint store. Her/his expertise could be very valuable in a case where a homeowner and a painting contractor are at odds over the quality, timing, or payment of a painting contract.

Furthermore, there is a greater likelihood that the example mediator and the painting contractor may have areas of commonality, whether as persons who may have had business contacts in the past, or may in the future, or whose relationship is that of past or future competitors.

Family and domestic mediators are probably more zealous in guarding against conflicts of interest. A family or domestic mediator whose spouse runs an insurance business should not mediate the divorce of the owner of a rival insurance business.

The admonitions about conflicts of interest extend into the future as well. Mediation trainers urge mediators to scrupulously avoid contact with either party under any circumstances in the

> An **inside mediator** means a mediator who has significant knowledge about the subject matter of the dispute. **Outside mediators** would be every mediator who is not an inside mediator.
> Sometimes, having a background in the subject matter can be helpful to understanding the dispute. Sometimes, it is not necessary. Having knowledge about the subtleties or nuances of a subject is not the same thing as being asked to use expertise to decide which version of something is correct. Remember: mediators do not decide—the parties do. The parties need to consider the possibilities and the importance of the differences.

months following the mediations. A lawyer who serves as a mediator is prohibited from representing either party in any further action even remotely connected with the original issues. A mediator who heard a dispute between a restaurant and an unhappy customer should not contact the restaurant management to cater the food for a reception.

Sometimes parties decide to return to mediation. When that happens, the mediators are very careful to keep all contacts even-handed and often revisit conflict of interest discussions.

Keep in mind, however, the mediator is not a judge, and will not be examining evidence or testimony for the purpose of determining whose **"facts"** are best or who should "win," or for issuing any judgment or ruling. Think of it this way: for the civil court system or arbitration to come to a conclusion about what the "correct" result is in any dispute, they must first find out what the "facts" are and then argue about how the facts fit into the law. Most of the rules and mechanics of court-room law practice are designed to create a system for testing the truthfulness of all of the parties "facts." What the parties claim are "facts," at the start of the process, are really not much more than their deeply held—but usually opposite—beliefs. Witnesses, records, documents, **evidence,** objections, rulings, hearsay, etc., are all devices that judges and lawyers use to give everybody a fair shot at proving up the "facts" that they believe are important. Sometimes, it is really important to get at the true facts. However, many times, the true facts either can't ever really be discovered or aren't quite as important to the parties as they are to the judge or the arbitrator. Mediation provides a way for parties to agree to avoid all of the court-room rules and processes (and expense) and

NUTS AND BOLTS

to form their own resolution, based upon what is important to them, that they both feel is just and right under their circumstances.

If, after conversations about conflict of interest, you are not comfortable with the mediator, self-determination gives you the power—and the responsibility—to speak up for your interest. You might decide to change mediators, that is, you might decide not to accept the mediator for your dispute. Be polite and be reasonable. In some formal mediation programs, there is likely a process for obtaining a substitute mediator. In less structured or informal settings, it may be more of a problem to obtain a substitute.

Mediator Competence

Unfortunately, there are not enough **peacemakers** in this world, but if you are involved in a disagreement, you can choose any peacemaker you are acquainted with to help tame the conflict.

> **Evidence** and **facts** are terms borrowed from court. So is **testimony.** In mediation, the parties will talk and express themselves about what they think is important—and some of what is said may appear to be based upon facts, testimony or evidence. However, the mediator is not present to decide who is right or what the facts are. No one is put "under oath" to give testimony or to present "facts" or "evidence." Remember, mediation differs from civil court and from arbitration in that, in mediation, the important "facts," "evidence" and "testimony" are what the parties "agree" they are. No more and no less. The parties have the power to agree on what is important to them in their mutual search for resolution.

The peacemaker you freely select is not required to be registered or approved or certified or licensed by any board. The only requirement is that the other party to the dispute must be willing to accept your choice—and the peacemaker must also agree to the effort.

Some people have a natural inclination, a knack, for being able to calm volatile situations, to restore order, to de-fuse anger. If you are not fortunate enough to know one of these rare individuals, you will want some assurance that the mediator handling your case has a demonstrated level of competence.

> Think of **peacemaker** as an umbrella word that includes not only mediators but anyone else who is willing to help resolve disputes through discussion. Peacemakers are regulated only by the parties. Mediators, especially mediators who hold themselves out as available for public mediation for payment, are regulated by the parties and, sometimes, by state or local governments.

There are several ways to reassure yourself that your mediator is minimally competent. Begin by asking questions directly. Reputable mediators are anxious to build trust, and will not be offended at the questions, especially if they are phrased in a courteous manner.

Information can often be obtained at the state level, although it may take a bit of searching. The growth of mediation from the ground up has resulted in a confusing array of commissions, boards, councils, agencies, departments, and private providers engaged in some form or aspect of mediation. Many also provide mediator training or certification.

Not too long ago, the word "mediation" couldn't be found in the yellow pages of any phone book. Some of the people who were practicing mediation had never heard of the word.

What these early mediators—who came from many different walks of life—had in common was a belief that there had to be a calmer, more humanizing manner of settling disputes than courtroom confrontations which—all too often—lead to permanently damaging, destructive outcomes.

It cannot be denied that the conflict resolution movement arose spontaneously in many different parts of the country. When the individuals who were pursuing goals of mediation began to communicate with each other, and to share experiences, the movement became more visible to outsiders.

The early practitioners became the first trainers. It is now possible to find courses and classes about mediation being taught in many diverse locations—some at educational institutions and some by private mediators.

Beginning mediators often improve their skills by serving internships in mediation programs, or by participating in co-mediations with seasoned individuals.

Competent mediators have a track record. Ask them. Ask them also if your state has an Alternative Dispute Resolution Commission or Board or a state mediator's association. They should be able to provide you with telephone numbers or website addresses.

> **ROADMAP—**
>
> Does all this seem like a maze? You can detour out of here to the specific chapters that interest you. Just don't forget how to get back!

Confidentiality

Confidentiality is one of the most hotly discussed aspects of mediation. Because the laws of the state where you live may explain or define confidentiality—and exceptions to confidentiality—in different ways, you should definitely ask questions of your mediator.

Expectation of confidentiality is what allows parties to freely exchange information and explore options for resolution. Confidentiality encourages open dialogue. If all of the parties know that alternatives considered, ideas and solutions suggested will remain inside the mediation, they may feel more free to try ideas out—to see if they might help reach a resolution.

Many mediations, whether with private mediators or in court-annexed programs, begin with the signing of a written "Agreement to Mediate." Confidentiality will be one of the areas covered in this document.

Exceptions to confidentiality should also be explained by the mediator at this time. Frequently, exceptions to the protection of confidentiality include information about potential abuse of children, elderly, or handicapped persons, or persons who are vulnerable because of diminished physical or mental capabilities. Laws may require disclosure or reporting of information about potential abuse. Neither can confidentiality be used to keep secret information about a crime or an expressed intent to commit a crime. Mediation cannot be used to hide information about potentially criminal activities.

Exceptions aside, virtually everything said or done during the process of mediation is to remain confidential.

Sometimes when a case is referred for mediation directly from the courtroom, as often happens in small claims courts, for example, one party will refuse outright to participate in mediation. When the mediator returns the file to the judge, never hope—or fear—that the mediator will pin the blame on the non-cooperative side. The mediator will be silent and will maintain confidentiality.

> **Confidentiality,** in terms of mediation, means: "What is said in mediation stays in mediation." That is, except for the parties' agreement, all of the discussions, the positions, the proposals, the conversations, the alternatives considered in mediation are not to be discussed outside of the mediation—by the parties and, especially, the mediator. Think of mediation as a very private—if sometimes emotional—conversation between the parties and the mediator.

But be wary of being the obstreperous party. Judges get to be judges by being very canny observers, and when they open the case for trial they will quickly be able to make their own assessment.

Whether the parties have freely entered into private mediation, or the case has arisen from a court proceeding, mediators guard against personal conflicts of interest. If the contemplated mediation is private, and the mediator discovers a conflict of interest, s/he simply refuses the case (perhaps with recommendations of other mediators to contact). If the fact that no mediation has taken place needs to be reported to the court, the mediator does just that: reports that no mediation has taken place. No reason should ever be given—that information is confidential, too.

Another layer of confidentiality will surround any short mini-sessions the mediator may have separately with each party. The mediator may refer to these individual conversations as a caucus, and all parties should be accorded approximately equal time for discussions with the mediator.

Information shared during a caucus is normally treated as confidential. What the parties impart in caucus usually—but not always—has a direct bearing on the matters in dispute.

If the mediator feels that revealing the information could be helpful in reaching resolution, the mediator may make that suggestion to the party. The party is in control of whether the information is to be revealed to the other party. Even when not revealed, the insight may still prove valuable to the mediator in helping to develop options as the mediation progresses.

No experienced mediator is ever surprised to hear during caucus things that are only remotely connected to the conflict. By far the greater numbers of remarks are complaints about the personality and the behavior of the other party. Less frequently, a party may want the mediator to hear and understand the overwhelming, but unrelated, pressures that have kept the party from dealing with the problem.

Although it's a stretch sometimes to connect opinions and recollections to the current issues, just having someone listen to your problems may help you get beyond the pain—or anguish or embarrassment or frustration—and enable you to reach a point where you are more capable of facing whatever brought you to the mediation.

Mediators will encourage each party to focus specifically on future solutions, but mediators are also acutely aware that sometimes it is vital to get some of the other baggage out of the way before real progress can be made.

After all the conversations and negotiations, if an agreement is finally stated in words, who will see the concluding document?

That depends.

In a private mediation, that determination will be made by the individuals who are the parties to the agreement. The parties, who have entered voluntarily into the mediation, have the final say—and this, too, must be by mutual agreement—about who will have access to the final agreement. That is: when and under what circumstances will their agreement be revealed to other people.

In some mediation settings, the parties are urged to have their agreement reviewed by their attorneys before signing the document. A signed writing can almost always be a binding agreement affecting legal rights and positions outside of the mediation.

The parties can waive confidentiality. This can be helpful if there are individuals outside of the mediation who may need to be informed so that the details of the agreement can be accomplished.

If you have been ordered by a judge to participate in a domestic or family mediation, any final agreement will probably be put in written form and submitted to the judge. The conversations, the dialogues, the exchanges, the options that were considered and rejected—all these are the parts that should remain confidential.

Practices differ from court to court, from state to state. Ask. Get clarification where needed. Make sure you understand your rights and your obligations of confidentiality.

Quality of the Process

Mediation trainers often remind mediators that the parties control the outcome, but the mediators control the process. It might be more accurate to say that mediators are responsible for the quality of the process while the parties are in control of the process.

The quality of the process depends largely on the mediator's ability to put aside distracting thoughts and focus on the concerns of the parties. The room where the sessions will be held should be free of distractions, without ringing phones or pagers. No one not involved in the mediation should have access to the room.

Mediators often move and speak in a calm, deliberative manner to try to assure the parties that no one will be rushed or pressured into making decisions. It's normal for mediators to establish simple ground rules: only one person talks at a time, no name-calling, no interruptions. The mediator's goal is to create an aura of fairness and impartiality and to build the kind of conversation or dialogue that makes resolution possible.

If circumstances permit, the mediator may ask the parties to establish conditions under which the mediation will be conducted. How long will they work before taking a break and what other rules of conduct do all parties think are important to observe?

The mediator will listen to all parties in a respectful manner, and will expect that the parties will do the same for each other.

All conflicts are emotionally charged, and not all hidden agendas will be brought to the table.

On the surface, the dispute may appear to be as simple as returning unsatisfactory goods to a merchant and getting a refund. Or, it may involve the multi-level differences between a couple whose marriage fell apart after the death of a child. Each mediation has its own twists and turns.

The mediator should always be prepared for displays of emotion that the parties find difficult to control, such as anger, dismay, frustration, embarrassment, regret, grief, sorrow—even hysteria or violence.

Caucus can be called for many reasons. One very good reason simply would be that of allowing the parties a break from each other. Once the parties have been separated from each other, the mediator will work to de-escalate emotions. If that's not going to be very successful, the mediator may shift into shuttle mediation mode. The parties will remain in separate rooms, and the mediator will carry information and offers of possible solutions from one party to the other. You may be familiar with the concept of shuttle mediation from watching the world news—it is often used in peace negotiations—think of "shuttle diplomacy"—and it can work. If advisable, the mediator may even suggest a **recess**—although recess and rescheduling are not always easy or advisable. Sometimes, perseverance—sticking to things until the work gets done—has its own rewards.

Mediation at a distance has also been used effectively. Parties who are at different geographic locations can agree to participate in conference calls. It helps keep blood pressure down if one party is not forced to be in the same room as the person who aggravates her/him more than anyone else in the world. It can also save a ton of travel time and expense.

Video conferencing is coming, but may never be used as widely as telephone conferencing. On video, you have to sit up straight, be sure your hair is neatly combed. On the telephone, only your voice is heard. No one knows—unless you mumble—that you are eating left-over pizza, and that you are still in your bathrobe, stretched out in your recliner chair.

Wherever, the mediator will be responsible for keeping the mediation moving forward. Most mediators are very persistent, and remain willing to stay with the process as long as there is any hope of a resolution.

The parties—this bears repeating—have total control of the outcome.

> **ROADMAP—**
>
> Still slogging through? You are persistent, but the good news is you're getting near the end of the explanations, and the last two are shorter!

Advertising and Solicitations

Mediators do not advertise heavily—for one thing, most of them do not make large sums of money. But not advertising does make them harder to find.

Advertisements offering mediation services "shall be truthful" and "refrain from promises and guarantees of results." How can an ethical mediator make a promise or a guarantee that there will be a successful result when the final decision is out of the mediator's hands? Remember: the mediators lead the process—the parties control the outcome.

Looking for a mediator? Start with the listings and other advertisements in telephone books. Some mediators practice solo, or you may find a name that indicates a group of mediators. The internet also has a lot of information—sometimes so much it can be confusing.

In most states—with few exemptions—you can find a commission or similar body whose function is to provide information about alternative dispute resolution. These groups are known by many different names. This is a clear testimony to the grassroots origin of the modern mediation movement, arising simultaneously in many different regions at more or less the same time.

Some of these organizations are prepared to provide the names of mediators who have met the training requirements in their state. Most lists of mediator names will also carry a disclaimer to the effect that "registration with the commission does not imply any degree of mediation skills or competency," or something along those lines. But not all states have training or credentialing requirements.

Pick out three or four names of mediators who are located near where you live and start making your inquiries.

Mediators are far less likely than other professions to be able to refer you to satisfied clients. After all, confidentiality and privacy are the very reasons that persons seek the services of a mediator in the first place. The mediator may have a brochure to send to you or a web-site listing, but it's no big deal if they don't.

Solicitation? What does that mean?

Solicitation is a word with a lot of meanings. Here, it just means that if a mediator offers to provide mediation services to you, s/he is held to the same standards as if they were placing an advertisement in a publication.

That means that someone who is offering

mediation services is required, ethically, to tell you the truth about her/his experience and expertise, and to be upfront about fees and charges.

If your research does not confirm that the advertisements of the mediator you have contacted are truthful, that no unrealistic results have been promised, or that no unreachable guarantees of success have been assured, go to the next name on your list.

Fees and Payments

The most burning issue is always:

"Are we going to find a resolution for our problem?"

But right after that comes anxiety about:

"How much is this going to cost?"

The cost of mediation (mostly a fee for the mediator's time and services)—and who pays and how much—is something that should be understood from the very beginning. Mediation may cost you nothing, or it may cost you a little bundle and still be worth every penny.

First, let's talk about no-cost, or low-cost, mediation.

If you live an in area served by a community or county mediation center, and if your dispute is about community or neighborhood issues unrelated to money, you may qualify for mediation services at no cost to either party.

Make that telephone call to find out.

Many community centers rely on volunteer mediators, receive grants and other resources from the community, and are very successful at fundraising. On the other hand, if the center has a hard time paying its utility bills, you may be charged a reasonable amount for the mediation services.

If you have been ordered by the court to participate in mediation, whether or not you will be charged may depend upon the services available in your judicial district. You'll have to ask. But make sure you do—before starting.

A good average, for most private mediations, will range from $75 to $150 per hour with a two-hour minimum. Some mediators will do a limited number of mediations for $25 to $60. If the dispute is complicated, involves more than two or three people, or revolves on a great deal of property or a large sum of money, the charge made by the mediator can range from $150 to $500 an hour.

Depends.

Don't hesitate to talk about it—ask questions. Make sure you understand what your obligations will be.

Very often the fee is split between the parties, each party paying half. Dividing the cost has an evening effect. Sometimes simple division is not possible, and under those circumstances, the cost may be based on a sliding fee scale.

On occasion, the first party is so relieved that the second party is willing to participate in mediation that s/he is prepared to pay the entire fee.

Most mediators expect to be paid in advance by

either cash or money order. Mediators have learned through hard experience to make this requirement. Too many mediators have been stuck with too many Non-Sufficient-Funds checks.

Depending on the type of mediation, many mediators schedule the first session for a two-hour period. Mediators are usually very generous with not billing for the time—which can be considerable—that they expend figuring out how to get everybody at the same place at the same time. It takes a lot of phone calls.

What is the ultimate cost if you decide against using mediation?

Unresolved issues can fester for a long time. Lawsuits can cost a lot of money. Think it through.

How much—of what—do you want to save?

A lawsuit can take unexpected sums of money out of your pocket. And untold hours out of your life. Lawsuits often cost more in emotional unrest and distress than in money or property loss.

A trial in a courtroom will alter and can damage any relationship. If you really do not expect to have any further transactions with the other party you may not be concerned about any damage.

But if you have a shred of a desire to diminish hard feelings as much as possible, mediation is your best choice.

> **ROADMAP—**
>
> Congratulations to all of you who have read this chapter all the way through. You may not have "mastered" all of the Nuts and Bolts of the mediation process, but you should have a better understanding now of what the process is about and how mediation should work for you. Remember: You Can Survive!
>
> Oh, you haven't read all of it yet? Well, just bookmark it so you can find your way back when you are ready!

YOUR BETTER JUDGMENT
(Getting Started)

Chapter Three

You wonder if you've lost your mind. Against your better judgment, you've agreed to mediation.

At the least, you are puzzled.

At worst ... scared.

What will the mediator "decide?"

Does your opponent know the mediator and does

s/he expect that to give her/him an advantage over you? Has the mediator already talked to your opponent?

Has the mediator heard the other party's story, and formed a negative opinion about you before you've even met?

Here is where you can begin to take control—you can ask any questions.

Fortunately, with a good mediator, at this point you probably won't have to ask much. The mediator will be assuring you that unless participation has been ordered by a court, mediation is an entirely voluntary procedure.

Try to stay cool and don't let any nervousness or emotions overpower you. The mediator will explain most of what you need to know without any questions from you. But don't be afraid to ask about anything you don't understand. After all, it is your mediation.

It may be your private opinion that the matter would not have reached such a serious stage if the other party had been willing to listen long enough to understand your point of view. To paraphrase one experienced small claims judge: many disputes arise because someone quit listening too soon.

To even the playing field, the mediator may set some ground rules. Or, you may be asked to help decide what the ground rules should be. Things like—no interrupting, no name-calling, no making faces or emitting rude sounds of disgust or disbelief.

And everyone will have an ample opportunity to speak.

Mostly common courtesies.

The "Golden Rule" is a pretty good guide to have in mind. Everyone knows some version: treat people the way you want to be treated.

Some mediators will provide notepads and pens which the parties can use to write down points they want to remember when it is their turn to talk. If note paper is not offered and you feel that making a note will be helpful, you can make your request with a silent gesture, such as pretending to write on the palm of your hand.

The mediator will listen, attentively and patiently, to all sides of the dispute. If you want to be fairly heard, naturally, you will have to return the favor.

Sometimes the rooms provided for mediation may be lacking in comfort, but the mediator—or mediators—will try to help everyone be as relaxed as possible.

Feeling comfortable may mean taking a break. Early on, the mediator will probably say something about taking a caucus, which simply means that the mediator will spend a few minutes talking with one party while the other party steps out of the room—and vice versa.

Who gets to take the first break? At least one mediator, (me), has an (almost) iron-clad rule about breaks. Unless someone has asked for a break, the party nearest the door leaves first. When s/he returns, the second party has a chance to stretch her/his legs, get a drink of water, or maybe go outside for some breaths of fresh air.

If you start feeling squirmy before the mediator wants to break for a caucus, just raise your hand with a silent time-out gesture and the mediator will quickly catch your drift.

It is a good idea, but not always required or necessary, to have a written agreement that the parties will submit their disputes to mediation.

> An **Agreement to Mediate** is NOT the same as the final, concluding **Mediation Agreement** although, unfortunately, they sure sound alike. The Agreement to Mediate is used to set out the starting point of the mediation while the Mediation Agreement is used at the end of the mediation to write down any resolution or conclusions that the parties have been able to reach in mediation.
>
> The need for a Mediation Agreement is discussed later on.

This preliminary **Agreement to Mediate** summarizes, in written form, the terms and conditions for the mediation to which both—or all—parties have agreed. The preliminary agreement should be a short (and hopefully simple) document. The actual wording will vary from mediator to mediator or from court to court. Sometimes, the parties may have included an agreement to submit their dispute to mediation as a term or condition of a different agreement—for example, a purchase agreement or a divorce settlement agreement.

Whether the Agreement to Mediate is a part of a separate agreement or is prepared specifically for the mediation, it would normally set out the names of the parties and the name of the mediator (or co-mediators) and may also generally describe the subject or topics that are going to be mediated. The document may also describe when and where the mediation will be held.

Make certain that any Agreement to Mediate describes anticipated or expected costs, if there are going to be any, and who is going to be responsible to pay them. It is best to also include a description of when that payment is going to be made. It is almost never a good idea to link responsibility for payment with "success" or "failure" in mediation. To aid the perception of impartiality, many parties agree (at least at this initial stage) to split mediation costs equally. Failure to decide who is to pay the costs of mediation could lead to more disputes, not less.

An Agreement to Mediate might also include information about who may be present at the mediation—for example, advisors, lawyers, family members—and what documents or outside materials might be brought to the mediation.

There is quite a range of thought about whether or how (or how much!) lawyers or other advisors should participate in the mediation process. In fact, while a great number of mediators are lawyers or are law-trained, there has been hostility—for whatever reasons—among judges and lawyers toward mediation. The answer to whether and how much lawyers or other advisors should be involved in or participate in the mediation is—and should be—entirely up to the parties. Advisors should not be present to discuss the dispute with the other party. It is often very difficult for advisors—whether lawyer, accountant or supportive spouse—not to engage in advocating or arguing for their client's position. It is not only in their nature but it is often part of what the client has hired them to do. However, most mediators will not permit direct conversation between advisors and the other party. Instead, caucus provides an excellent time for advisors to advise their clients about developments, proposals and possible resolutions without direct conversation with the other parties. Simply: mediators should mediate, advisors should advise, and the parties should make all of the decisions.

> **!! Lawyers in Mediation:** Wise lawyers (and most judges) see mediation for what it is—or might be—to the parties: a cost-effective way for a client to have a say and control in finding resolution to important disputes—without the cost or emotional expense of trial and pre-trial preparations. Every case resolved by mediation also helps clear over-crowded court dockets. With even small trials of simple cases potentially costing thousands of dollars for every party, mediation is almost always a reasonable alternative. !!

The best rule-of-thumb for what should be included in an Agreement to Mediate is that anything about the mediation process or procedure that is (or seems to be) important to any of the parties and that is agreeable to all of the other parties can be included. If something—anything—is important to you (remember your control through the exercise of your right of self-determination!) you need to be strong enough to ask to have the issue addressed. If it is really important to one of the parties and can be agreed to by all of the parties, it should be addressed. However, don't bog mediation down worrying with unnecessary details of rules, conditions or procedures.

An Agreement to Mediate should never include a commitment or requirement to reach an agreement. While parties may be required to participate in mediation, they cannot be required (that is—they cannot be forced or ordered) to reach any agreement in mediation.

Most Agreement to Mediate documents contain phrases to the effect that the parties will not be able to ask the mediator to appear in court at some later time in connection with the dispute. This is an effort to protect confidentiality.

There are limits to confidentiality, as seen above. Additionally, the parties can agree to waive confidentiality so that the outcome (the concluding Mediation Agreement) can be shared with persons outside of the mediation. Any such waiver of confidentiality can be in either the Agreement to Mediate or the Mediation Agreement but should always be put in writing.

> ‼ There is a great deal of difference between, on one hand, being required to participate in a mediation effort (which is sometimes done by courts or legislatures and is well within the boundaries of mediation), and, on the other hand, being required to reach an agreement in mediation—which is NOT mediation but is a lot closer to what is called binding arbitration. In fact, the two are opposites—one gives the parties control over whether and on what terms they might reach a voluntary resolution to their dispute and the other takes away the power of self-determination. ‼

The serious responsibility of preserving the conditions regarding confidentiality weighs more heavily on the mediator than it does on the parties. The details of the dispute should never become fuel for gossip between the mediator and the butcher, baker or candlestick maker or banker, barber, auto-mechanic or kids' league soccer coach. However, there are limits to confidentiality, as discussed in Chapter Two, the Nuts and Bolts chapter.

Before the mediation actually starts, take a deep breath, relax against the back of your chair, and ask yourself if all your questions about the procedure have been answered. If not, speak up for yourself! But, it is possible that some of the mediator's responses may not become clear until later. So, take another deep breath or two, settle comfortably into your seat, and commit yourself to explore the process.

Mediation is not a trap.

Mediation is voluntary, remember. Even when mediation has been ordered by a court, only your attendance is necessary to comply with the order.

Even though it may be in the best interests of the parties, the judicial order does not command the parties to reach a decision. You cannot be ordered to "agree" in mediation. However, a wise judge knows that the parties have a greater knowledge of their circumstances than anyone else, and is willing to put the power to decide fate in their own hands. No less than Solomon was such a judge.

As a participant, your job is to offer your proposals for resolution, at the same time listening with a cautious ear to consider the other party's suggestions.

YOUR BETTER JUDGMENT

If the proposals are in direct conflict, and mediation has reached **impasse,** the mediator may offer other ideas.

The mediator's suggestions will likely be prefaced by an explanation. Perhaps something like "In a different case, with somewhat similar circumstances, the parties were willing to consider ... these options, etc."

Or, "do you think any of these ideas—which have helped resolve the conflicts for other persons—might work for you?" the mediator might ask.

The mediator's ideas are something you can look at and reject—or accept. They are designed to be food for thought and fuel for resolution. They are not a decision or an order.

It is important to keep in mind that, while mediators may put ideas or suggestions on the table for consideration, mediators are not there to give you or anyone else "advice" about what to do.

> **Impasse** means that the parties cannot agree on a resolution. They are at loggerheads—a stand-off. But remember, impasse is a temporary condition and the parties have the power to end impasse—if they want to. Mediation is designed to let parties explore alternatives to impasse. Explore away! Conversation and dialogue is almost always one of the least expensive parts of any conflict.

At the beginning of a mediation, the parties usually address their remarks directly to the mediator. Each party is acutely aware of the other party's presence, but each may make a conscious effort to not turn, or even look, in the other's direction.

Frequently, as the process continues, the parties will turn more often toward each other. Occasionally, the discussion will become a two-party dialogue, to the exclusion of the mediator. Unless the remarks become too acrimonious, good mediators often just go with the flow.

If, however, the parties' emotions escalate and the atmosphere becomes too intense, the mediator may call for a break or caucus. Sometimes, the mediator will direct the parties to separate rooms, and instead of bringing the parties together again, the mediator will move back and forth from one to the other.

Between themselves, mediators call this method "shuttle mediation," and experience shows that agreements can still be reached even when parties are extremely hostile toward each other.

Mediation should never feel rushed. The door should always remain open to a temporary recess. On occasion it may become apparent that either party—or both—needs time to gather information they did not bring with them. It could be that the whole process would run more smoothly following a "cooling off" period of a few days or a even a couple of weeks.

As the mediation moves along, the mediator probably will be taking notes, and will refer to the notes if a concluding agreement has been reached.

If the parties are able to reach resolution, it is best to reduce their agreement to a written concluding agreement—the **Mediation Agreement.** There are few formal requirements for such an agreement. It can take almost any form the parties wish, as long as the proposed actions are not illegal. In fact, actual Mediation Agreements can be downright inventive. They range from notes on the proverbial cocktail napkin (not always the best idea!) to multi-page formal statements. These might include sentences describing an agreement for the payment of money, a delivery of property, the performance of services, maybe even the expression and acceptance of a heartfelt apology.

People are often surprised to discover how many disputes are resolved through the power of apology and acceptance of responsibility and the reconciliation that sometimes results.

The concluding Mediation Agreement should be written in straight-forward language, free of legalese. The wording is quite likely to use some of the same language actually expressed by the parties.

All the necessary details, as agreed upon by the parties, should be included. For example, if one party has agreed to pay money to the other party, the exact terms of how and when the payment will be made should be included. A schedule of payments which will be made in the future should be listed.

How, when and where the payments will be made should be a part of the Mediation Agreement. By personal check? By money order? On what dates? In person? By mail? To home address? To business address? To an intermediary?

The legal community would argue that before you sign a Mediation Agreement, you should have the document reviewed by an attorney, but that's a call you can make yourself. Know that the Mediation Agreement will likely affect the legal rights and obligations for one or all of the parties.

What will happen to the concluding Mediation Agreement? Well, both—or all—parties should take home a copy. If the mediation has been done with a private mediation service, the mediator may keep a copy in her/his files. Or maybe not.

When the mediation has taken place through a community mediation center, it's likely that a copy will be kept in the center's files.

Practices differ in programs which are offered through small claims courts. In some jurisdictions, the judge wants to know only that a Mediation Agreement was reached; if the parties do not comply with the conditions of the agreement, and the case returns to the courtroom, the judge may want to hear the case "as if for the first time."

In other small claims courtrooms, immediately following the close of the mediation, the mediator and the parties will appear before the bench where the judge will read the agreement. If s/he finds the terms acceptable, the judge will make the Mediation Agreement the Court's Order.

Often, towards the end of a mediation, things tend to get a little rushed. In their minds, the parties have reached an agreement, are impatient with the concluding details, and are already thinking about what they are going to do next.

That's still not a good excuse for not clarifying any questions you might have. If you think you need to know who will have a copy of the Mediation

Agreement, or what the judge will or will not do with your agreement, slow things down until you get an answer to all of your questions. Be absolutely certain that you understand everything that you have agreed or committed yourself to do. Also, of course, make certain that you understand what the other parties have agreed to do as their part of the resolution.

Not all mediations conclude with agreements. It is, after all, a process that is based on the self-determination of the parties.

One alternative for parties who have not achieved what they hoped for in mediation is litigation. And the party who is unable—for whatever reason—to agree with what the other person wants should be forewarned that their next meeting may take place in a courtroom.

There are only two outcomes to every dispute: either it will be resolved, or it will go away. Most don't just go away. Mediation offers you a great deal of control over how the dispute will be resolved. Neither the court system nor arbitration offer the control of self-determination.

Mediators begin each session with the expectation that there will be an agreement, but they don't usually keep a scorecard for themselves.

They know that people can be stubborn, and some will cut off their own noses to save face.

The neighbor who refuses during mediation to agree to do anything about her/his tree limbs which are hanging over another neighbor's driveway may be out in the yard the next day trimming the offending branches.

The auto repair-shop owner may deny any responsibility for a theft from a customer's car that remained overnight on the shop premises, but next week may order the installation of a security-system for the building and grounds.

A caterer may not be willing to admit that a wedding cake s/he produced was something less than perfect, even if s/he knows in her/his own mind that the whole thing leaned like the Tower of Pisa. But for darned certain, the next cake that leaves her/his bakery will be double-checked for appearance and presentability.

And there are those mediation sessions that end in a very amicable fashion with nothing written on paper, only friendly nods or a handshake. Everyone has had a chance to be heard, the air has cleared, each party has a better understanding of the other's concerns, and everybody knows what they have to do to maintain a cordial relationship.

A lawyer colleague of mine professes to not understand mediation. *"I don't see how mediation can possibly work—it has no teeth in it."*

It works because people are most interested in their own self-interests. It works because when people have made a determination of what actions would be in their best interests, they are most likely to willingly follow that course of action.

Just remember: **Self-Determination!**

CONTROLLING THE SPLIT
(Mediation in Divorce)

Chapter Four

WARNING!

If you need this chapter, please be forewarned. The going gets tough. As you will come to know, this chapter will be a lot easier to read than it is to live through the reality of divorce. But stick with it—you want the best results for your children and yourself. And mediation is likely to be a part of those results.

Many courts order participation in mediation as a part of the divorce process.

Prepare yourself ahead of time. Don't allow yourself to be blind-sided because you aren't willing to do a little advance thinking and preparation. The sports psychologists call it visualization—but the process is not new and not limited to sports. Think ahead. Be prepared. Have in mind what you think is good and right and fair.

The anger that accompanies the break-up of a family does not easily or quickly go away.

It matters not the form in which the anger is expressed. It can be open and raging. It can be suppressed and seething. Open anger can injure other persons. Suppressed anger can injure you.

If you choose to use mediation to work out new arrangements, or you are referred to mediation by a court, your first task will be to control your anger. Anger can change how you view possibilities. Don't let your anger get in the way of making life-altering decisions.

If it's a couple who are going their separate ways, aside from the emotional fall-out, the primary issues are who gets what. If it's a family that is being divided, the stakes are infinitely higher.

When divorce or post-divorce family cases come to court, the parties often are ordered to go to mediation to create a parenting-plan for the children. Behind closed doors, mediators debate amongst themselves how people can be ordered to participate in an activity that is described as voluntary. The general consensus is that while parties can be ordered to make a good faith effort to participate in mediation, they cannot be ordered to agree to a resolution.

Beyond that esoteric argument, mediators are dedicated to helping people find peaceful solutions, so when parties are mandated to mediation, mediators work very hard to help the parties understand that if they do participate in mediation, the parties will be the persons who will make their own decisions.

The flip side, refusing to be cooperative in mediation, is that a judge, who knows you impersonally as only one of hundreds of cases, only as names on a case file, will be making decisions and signing orders that will govern major areas of your life. Sometimes for a while.

Giving in to your anger will only weaken you.

Dread.

You may dread the idea of mediation. You may want to put it out of your thoughts. Don't. Grab hold of the process and plan to use it to your advantage. Those of us who believe in mediation, also believe it is the best and most useful way for you to have the greatest say in the outcome of the process. But you have to stay in control of your emotions and participate. Use your rights and powers of self-determination in mediation.

Before you start the mediation, ask what can be decided in mediation. In some court-connected domestic mediations, the mediators are allowed to facilitate only the decisions about child custody. The judge will follow court-developed formulas for ordering financial support.

Other programs will permit the court-connected mediators to cover all issues, including financial, in the mediation.

Private mediators, likewise, can encourage the parties to tackle all the relevant issues, financial as well as custody matters.

Take a lot of time to think about what you really want. Then do some more thinking about what would happen if you were to get the things you want. If you are really honest with yourself, you will admit that getting what you think you want could have its downside, too.

Now comes the truly difficult part of any mediation. Try to put yourself into the mind of the other party, your ex- (or soon to be ex-) spouse, and try to imagine what s/he might be seeking from her/his side. And what would be the long-range results if your (ex-) spouse gets what s/he wants? There could be an upside for you.

Everything short of having your (ex-)spouse fall off the planet requires serious thought.

Have I made that too strong?

Once you enter the divorce arena, you lose control over some of the most important parts of your life. From now on, until your youngest child reaches eighteen (and under some circumstances longer than that) the court will have the authority to issue orders about how you will live your life. One of the few ways to increase your hope for control over parts of the process is to make wise use of mediation alternatives.

If you are fortunate, your case will be heard by an

empathetic judge. It is equally likely that you may draw a judge who is more difficult to convince regarding the worthiness and reliability of your claims. And it is a virtual certainty that more than one judge, over the years, will hold the power of the gavel over what most people consider private circumstances of their lives.

It is going to be hard, but try focusing on the kids. If you can put the childrens' needs first, you will be taking the high road and setting a good example that your (ex-)spouse would be well advised to follow. You can bet that when the judge looks at any agreement you come up with, s/he will be looking for arrangements that are in the best interests of the children.

There are no perfect solutions. But workable solutions can be found. You can set the tone by making it very clear that your long-range goals are providing for your children's future. If you can keep the needs of your children uppermost in your mind, not only will you survive, they will survive in the best way possible under the circumstances.

The biggest decision is where the children will live. Every kind of time-sharing arrangement you can come up with probably has been tried already. If the children are small, the availability of trustworthy, convenient daycare may be a key element. When they start school, the location of the school will be of paramount importance.

No matter how bad the marriage may have become, there was probably some sharing of responsibility for the children, some commitment of time, so that neither parent was solely responsible for everything that happened to the children. And neither parent was solely in charge of determining what was good or best for the children.

Twenty-four hours a day, seven days a week, responsibility for children is quite a stretch. Much as you love them, they can wear down your patience.

With the best of intentions, parents may start out with a fairly equal sharing of time. When the children are old enough to begin attending school, it eventually makes more sense for the children to have their primary residence where the school is located.

That would mean, of course, that they will be spending more nights with one parent than the other. That may not necessarily add up to more quality time. In fact, it may be a more difficult task for that parent, who has to be prepared with food for breakfast, have the right change on hand for lunch money, send the children off properly clothed, and arrange their transportation—at the same time getting her/himself off to work. After school, it's homework time, another meal, and the never-ending protests about bed-time.

The parent who has the children on the weekends has considerable more hours for fun and activities. There is no bus to be caught, no ringing of the school bells.

But for as long as it lasts, it's 24/7.

Supplemental child care is a lot harder to find on a weekend.

After the basic living arrangements are determined, the next issues to tackle are providing for shared time during school breaks and holidays. What will be the trade-offs?

If the kids are with Dad for Thanksgiving, where will they be at Christmas? Which set of grandparents will be present for the gift openings and which will be left with unopened packages under the tree?

Decisions about Mother's Day and Father's Day and Dad's birthday and Mom's birthday are no-brainers, but what about the children's birthdays?

This is getting hard.

Underlying all these arrangements is the question of who is going to pay the bills, and how?

At some point you may have been asked to fill out a financial questionnaire. Most states use formulas to determine how much each parent will contribute to the care of their children.

Often the parent with the more secure employment, or the higher-paying job, will be able to add the children to their health insurance package.

Keep in mind that it is the judge who signs the court orders. If the parties can present a workable plan which they have agreed to either by themselves or through mediation, the judge will probably agree to their choices and sign the plan or the Mediation Agreement as an order of the court.

Note the word "probably." The judge's primary obligation is to look out for the welfare of the children. You might think it reasonable that your (ex-) spouse have the children on the day after Christmas of every third year, and that otherwise the children will live with you in a highway construction shack. It's doubtful that any judge would see eye-to-eye with you.

If the parties fail, for whatever reason, to reach an agreement that the judge finds reasonable, the judge will designate a plan. The judge's custody schedule, or decisions, will be based on arrangements that have worked for other families, but it will not be custom-tailored to fit the needs of your family and your children.

Do you want a "rubber-stamp" applied to your life?

Of course not!

Mediation, if you handle it right, can keep the decision-making power in your hands—and the hands of your (ex-)spouse.

When you think the mediation is finished, don't be too quick to sign the Mediation Agreement. You should have the opportunity to have your agreement reviewed by a lawyer.

Rick Epstein, the author of many books and columns about family relationships, writes:

"A good childhood is the one, big, everlasting gift that parents give a child."

This is your big chance. Don't blow it. You can put mediation to work for you—and your children—if you are willing to do some work.

HEALING THE HURT
(Mediation after Crime: Finding Solace)

Chapter Five

Victim/Offender mediation is not one-size-fits-all.

But it can provide some stepping stones toward healing, for both the victim AND the offender.

If you have been a victim, you may have a ton of questions. Why were you the target of the crime? How did you become the victim? Were you chosen randomly, or did the perpetrator pick you out, follow you, stalk you, and deliberately plan to harm you? And what becomes of the offender?

How serious is the damage that was done? Is the damage repairable? Or are the consequences irreversible? Material damage can be repaired, but the memories are never totally erased and can rush back to the forefront of the mind at unexpected times.

The scariest question of all—what is the identity of the person who harmed you?

Victim/Offender mediation is not available everywhere. Where it does exist, the program usually depends upon mediators who volunteer their time. Victim/Offender mediation organizations work closely with the courts.

Under most circumstances, if you are the victim, you can choose whether or not you want to participate. Don't rush through this decision—listen to the mediators as they explain the entire process to you.

Will you ever be left alone with the offender? If you need support, will you be allowed to bring someone with you? Who will be allowed to know what was said during the mediation? Suppose the offender just won't agree to anything?

The mediators who contact you should be willing to take all the time needed to help you feel less uneasy or less fearful about the process. They will try to avoid rushing you into a decision, although they may be required to work within court-imposed deadlines.

If at any point you are feeling overwhelmed, you can back out. Self-determination applies to

Victim/Offender mediation just as much as in all other forms.

There have been some high-profile televised meetings—inappropriately described as mediations—between victims and convicted criminals. Meetings and confrontations are not mediation. In the best of circumstances, the preliminary planning that took place before these meetings covered a period of many months. In cases like these, where the consequences of the crime are irreversible, the victims have spent many hours with mediators, counselors, psychiatrists, court personnel, ministers, family members and friends, anyone who could help them decide whether they wanted to continue with the process.

Be assured that public encounters of this kind are extremely rare, and will occur only with the full consent of the victim. In fact, it will only take place when virtually everyone who has been involved in the advance preparations is convinced that an informed consent has been given by the victim, and the victim is fully prepared for the encounter.

By far the most common practice is to surround the mediation with as much confidentiality as possible. This confidentiality will also cover some events outside the mediation sessions, events such as pre-mediation conversations with the mediators. Only the people who need to be involved will be informed.

Don't hesitate to ask questions at any point.

The victim who agrees to participate in Victim/Offender mediation wields a huge control. If the victim is uneasy about being in the presence of the offender, s/he can choose to have someone come to the mediation with her/him. That person might be a family member, a friend, an attorney or clergy. Anyone who is present in a supportive position should expect to play a passive role. The mediators will direct their questions and comments toward the parties, encouraging them to speak for themselves.

Within practical limitations, the choice of the victim also will determine the place for the mediation. Low-funded mediation programs notoriously have to fight for space. If there is an actual mediation center, a building or suite, something more expansive than a single office, there may be rooms available for private discussions.

Even if that option is available, the victim may choose to meet elsewhere. For some, a library study room might provide a zone of neutrality. A conference room in a church might give others the level of comfort necessary to allow the mediation to proceed. Even more reassuring to a victim who has felt truly threatened would be a mediation conducted in a police department.

The pace of the mediation will be kept under control. The mediator will be observing the parties closely, especially the victim, and will be quick to call a temporary—maybe even permanent—halt if the emotions become too intense.

The victim will have the option of stopping at any point. The mediators will help the victim decide whether to take a short break, or continue the mediation to another day.

You may be the offender who has been asked to participate in mediation. So, what's in it for you? Your position is admittedly difficult, but you can still exercise a significant amount of control.

For starters, you could refuse to participate. Be aware, however, and do not refuse until you've spent some time considering the alternatives to refusing.

Your initial response may be doubt, hesitation, shame, guilt, fear, anger. Whatever emotions you are feeling, your willingness to meet the person you have harmed will set a good tone at the very beginning.

By the time the mediators talk with you, they already know that the victim is willing to meet with you. Before you agree, ask all the questions that come to your mind. What are the limits of confidentiality? Ask about any fees. Get an assurance from the mediators that they will not be using coercive tactics to pressure you into making an agreement you do not want to make.

The mediation will not happen if the victim does not wish to participate, and the mediators will spend whatever preparation is necessary with the victim. It's quite likely that separate sessions also will be held with the offender. One of the decisions that will be explored will be the staying power of the offender, who will also have the power to bring the mediation to a halt.

As the offender, you may be thinking that you do not have much "wiggle" room.

Your options will depend on where your case is in the system. If you are a "first offender" this will be a good opportunity to make this your last offense.

If the mediation sessions have been recommended as part of a pre-judgment procedure, your ability or your willingness to make amends may well have a bearing on the judge's decision when your case is heard.

Victim/Offender mediation is sometimes called restorative justice. While no one believes that it would ever be possible to completely return to the past, a goal of mediation is to give the parties an opportunity to undo, in so far as is humanly possible, some of the damage and harm that has been done.

Often "first offender" mediations involve young people who have very limited resources. If the cost of the damage has been very high, as can sometimes happen in cases of vandalism, not only is it unreasonable, it may be impossible for a young offender to make full restitution.

If an agreement is reached and put into writing it should be mutually agreeable to all parties involved. No one—neither offender nor victim—should sign an agreement under pressure. No one should ever be coerced to sign a Mediation Agreement.

Most commonly, the written Mediation Agreement is signed at the close of the last session. Nonetheless, under some circumstances, the parties may ask, or may be urged, to review the document with their attorney prior to signing.

What can the document say? What does it need to say to start undoing the damage?

The goal is restoration, or restitution, both big words. Hopefully, there will be some level of conciliation.

There's a legend about how the whole Victim/Offender movement got started. It's a story that may be one of those modern-day myths that never actually happened, but it has been told enough times to believe it holds some elements of truth.

The tale involves a frustrated juvenile case worker. Why was s/he frustrated? Who knows exactly what impelled the case worker to take a totally unexpected step. Was the case worker disappointed because the young people s/he was working with displayed no remorse? Was it anger because the system made it appear that the juveniles' actions resulted in impersonal, victimless crimes against the state? Was s/he confounded because the offenders never seemed to realize how the consequences of their actions had impacted the lives of real people?

So what happened?

The case worker took the young people back to the neighborhood where they had vandalized a home. Standing on the sidewalk in front of the house, the case worker issued an order:

"I want you to go knock on that door, and when the people who live there open the door, I want you to tell them that you are sorry for what you did."

Nowadays, no experienced mediator would ever demand an apology from the offender. An apology might be healing for the victim, but if it is forced from the offender, it can create a lingering resentment. *But that case worker started a conversation. And the conversation proved helpful enough that it started a movement.*

When the mediator opens the mediation session, the first opportunity to speak will probably be given to the victim. What the victim says can provide clues about how the offender can make amends. While a monetary offer cannot erase emotional injuries, an offer of a payment can go a long way to repair property damage. And a genuine apology can have value that cannot be measured in money.

True mediation is never a one-way street. After the victim's time to speak, the offender will also have an opportunity to be heard. In fact, the victim may be eager to learn what impelled the offender to behave in a way that caused injury to another.

Perhaps the offender did not act alone, but had been persuaded by others. Maybe the consequences were unintended, an unfortunate accident as opposed to deliberate vandalism. Whatever the reason, the offender should be listened to respectfully.

The victim needs to be realistic in her/his expectations about receiving a payment. Sometimes the cost of replacement, or the repair of acts of vandalism, or other damage to property, can reach astronomical sums of money.

Understandably, some offenders—especially the young or unemployed—usually do not have either the money, or hopes of future earning power, to repay large amounts of money. Very young offenders have no means of earning money with which to pay for damages.

If a total financial repayment is not possible, perhaps both victim and offender should consider a partial payment, combined with some other type of recompense.

HEALING THE HURT

If you are the victim, be practical but not greedy about the financial repayment you hope to recover. If the offender could pay you back in every material way, would you still think something was missing?

As the victim, besides thinking about what more you can do to protect yourself in the future, you have probably looked at the larger picture and wondered if anything could be done to curb violence. Besides the debt the offender owes to you, is there some way the offender can make some contribution to society?

If you are the offender, be generous, but not overly optimistic about what you can offer. Do not offer an amount of money beyond your resources, or your ability to repay in a relatively short period of time.

The person who has suffered from the consequences of your actions may have in mind some kind of community service you could perform. It might be more to your favor if you have a suggestion that you can bring forward. You might offer to keep the lawn at the community center mowed for the summer. You could show a willingness to help serve food at a homeless shelter. Any suggestion on your part will demonstrate that you are aware of the needs of others.

The mediator will be willing to work as long as necessary to help the parties develop options and reach an agreement. If the parties appear to be stuck, not able to move forward, the mediator may suggest a "cooling off" period and a return to mediation at a later time.

If there is truly an impasse, the mediator will be rummaging through her/his mental bag of strategies in search of something that will stimulate a continuing conversation. If the parties are not able, with the help of the mediators, to generate options that are acceptable to both, there will be no agreement.

If this happens, the only thing the mediators will report to the court is that the mediation took place, but no agreement was reached. The mediators will share no comments with the court about what happened in the mediation sessions. S/he should never convey to the court her/his belief that the failure to reach an agreement was due to stubborn, or vengeful, or mean-spirited behavior by one or both of the parties.

What are the chances of an apology?

A sincere apology?

Expressions of regret shown by the offender will go a long way to help the victim move past the injuries.

Will the victim forgive the offender? Forgiveness, like an apology, has to come from the heart.

Both an apology and forgiveness may seem timid, hesitant, and tentative. But they can be shown to have tremendous curative power.

Expressions of apology and forgiveness can be written into the final document—or maybe not, depending entirely on the parties.

Recovery is something that takes time.

THEM AIN'T NO SMALL POTATOES
(Mediation not Litigation)

Chapter Six

There are all sorts of estimates about the number of legal cases that get filed at the courthouse but never reach the courtroom.

Somewhere along the line an agreement is reached and the parties never find themselves giving testimony in front of a judge. But they still use up your resources.

Lawsuits can drag out for years. Some hang around long enough to grow beards. And the longer they go, the more they cost.

Often the mere financial risk—large though it may be—is far outweighed by the emotional damage of a lawsuit that drags on ... and on ... and on ....

The uncertainties loom like ugly thunderclouds that never go away. How much will it cost? How many days will I lose? When will my case be scheduled to go before a judge? How many times will the court date be rescheduled?

And the biggest question of all?

WILL I WIN OR WILL I LOSE?

If you feel that another person has harmed you in some way, you usually have the power to decide how you will seek retribution. If you feel a lot of anger surrounding the issues you may be thinking more in terms of revenge.

If, instead of being a plaintiff seeking retribution (or revenge), you find yourself being named a defendant, you may be feeling more like a victim.

Keep reading. Mediation is an equal-opportunity process; it applies equally to both plaintiff and defendant.

Few people attempt to navigate their way through a district court case by themselves. Don't ever try to out-guess your attorney, but don't be afraid of doing your own legal research.

Take a day off to visit the courthouse where your case would be heard. Try to sit in the public gallery for a trial. Ask for directions to the law library. Law libraries are usually paid for and supported by the legal community, but they are often open to the general public.

Law libraries, with aisle after aisle of legal volumes, can be rather intimidating. You might be more comfortable browsing the shelves of self-help legal books at a public library, or a good book store. Also, there is a tremendous amount of legal information, even whole libraries, available through the internet—most of them free of charge.

Let your attorney do the job for which you hired her/him, but if you show yourself to be a knowledgeable listener, s/he will have more respect for you as a client.

> **ROADMAP—**
>
> Your research should show you that there are multiple avenues for reaching an outcome to any dispute:
>
> negotiation
>
> mediation   arbitration
>
> litigation
>
> war
>
> Developing resolution is like a road trip, and there is a good likelihood that you will find yourself on a different route.

Strong advice: Don't skip a trip to the courthouse. If you familiarize yourself with the courtrooms as an uninvolved, casual observer, you'll have more confidence when you have to be present to protect your own interests.

If you find an interesting trial to watch, take along a good book to read (for example, a self-help legal guide). Courtroom procedures seem to move in fits and starts. The army sometimes says hurry-up-and-wait. They mean it.

A change in route might be suggested by either attorney—or suggested or ordered by the judge—or you, yourself, might decide on an itinerary that may provide a smoother ride.

Litigation, of all the options, is almost always the most costly, the most time-consuming and the most demanding of everyone's emotions. It has its uses.

In some cases, arbitration can provide the best outcome—but that can depend on who gets to define what is "best" and how much control the parties are willing to give up in order to get to a resolution. Arbitrations are conducted by a formalized set of rules. Both parties are heard by an arbitrator, or a panel of arbitrators, and the decision can be either binding or non-binding.

Before you enter into arbitration, you should have a clear understanding whether the results will be binding or non-binding. Parties in dispute can agree to participate in arbitration, or they can be ordered to arbitration by the courts or, in a growing number of situations, legislatures. While scrupulous arbitrators try to be fair and impartial, the decision-making power is in the hands of the arbitrator and not the parties. One or both parties may be unhappy with the result.

Mediation, being a far more informal and more flexible procedure, is less rigidly defined. Nonetheless, the unyielding bedrock of mediation is the parties' **self-determination.** The parties should make their own decisions, unpressured and uncoerced.

In the end, both parties may not get all they want or were after, and they may not be deliriously happy with the agreement, but they will have had the opportunity, without coercion, to create the best agreement under the circumstances.

There are numerous other forms of alternative dispute resolution, and although the conclusion may provide satisfactory results, they should never

> **Alternative dispute resolution,** often referred to as ADR, is used to identify pretty much every form of solving disputes outside of the legal system's courtroom and civil lawsuit process. Not all ADR methods are the same and not all have equal application or purpose. In addition to mediation, the "gold standard" of ADR, some disputes are put through:
> **negotiation,**
> **arbitration,**
> **reconciliation,**
> **facilitation,**
> **neutral evaluation,**
> **settlement conference,**
> **family-circle conferencing** or, in some instances,
> **administrative law hearings** (formal or informal) or a panel or hearing process—such as a medical evaluation board. In each, the goal is to find or force a resolution without a courtroom trial.

be confused with mediation. Not everybody is always looking at the same road map.

The courts look very favorably at the possibilities of conciliation. Reconciliation is also used as an almost synonymous term—for many people the two terms have the same meaning. Generally, the process implies restoring a damaged relationship to a previously congenial or compatible condition. A mini-trial is presented, not to an abbreviated jury of six persons, but to a panel chosen by both parties. A neutral third-party is included as a panel member. Unless the parties agree in advance, the recommendations of the panel are non-binding, but often provide both parties information upon which to base settlement offers.

Neutral evaluation—in some states there is a process in which both parties agree to ask for a neutral assessment of the merits of their claims. This is also described as an early neutral evaluation. The neutral person performing the evaluation provides an independent recommendation concerning options for settlement.

Settlement—a term hard to pin down—is what the judges hope for when they think of ADR. To understand that their job is to get court cases to their end is to understand what judges are looking for. Judges are far less comfortable with the forms of ADR that do not conclude with a specific agreement. Judges hope for a paper and ink document that they can sign as an order of the court—this puts an end to the case that is in front of them. Sometimes judges try to get a settlement by requiring the parties to participate in an informal "settlement conference" where alternative positions and posturings are explored by the attorneys and parties. In other instances (usually big cases and big disputes) a summary jury trial may be conducted under the direction of the court and is presided over by a judge. Witnesses are not usually heard, and attorneys are given a time-limit to present their arguments. The decision of a six-person jury is non-binding, but serves as an indication of what might happen if the case were to go to trial before a full jury. The decision often can serve as a basis for settlement of the conflict.

Look for ADR—alternative dispute resolution—on the internet, and you'll find a bewildering array, including also facilitation, moderated settlement conference, family-circle conferencing, and a hybrid, mediation-arbitration. A diligent search can undoubtedly find even more types of ADR—sometimes being offered as a commercial product under a brand name.

It's hard for a professional from another state to explain each category in detail, so ask questions whenever you get a chance—and whenever it matters to your dispute.

None of the other alternatives empower the parties as much as mediation. Of all the forms of ADR, mediation—especially the transformative style—is probably the more user-friendly.

Mediation allows you to take ownership of the dispute. Instead of sitting silently while a judge and the lawyers discuss your life and talk about your dispute, you can describe your view of the important facts and circumstances in your own words to the mediator and the other party. Instead of mentally squirming while you hear what other parties say about you from the witness stand in front of a cast of strangers, you are reassured that you will have equal time to express your views in your own words.

Along the way, you will have to do your share of the listening. Ditto for your opposition.

There is no single mediation style. Some mediators will want to keep the mediation participants in the same room for the entire session. Other mediators believe mediation works best if the caucus model—or style—is used in which the mediator will meet separately with each individual at least once and maybe several times during the actual session.

There are some circumstances for which a shuttle style is most effective—and there are some mediators who much prefer this method. All of the parties are gathered together for at least a brief introductory session before the parties are directed to separate areas. Then the mediator moves from room to room, carrying messages and suggestions of how the dispute might be resolved between the parties.

When is mediation appropriate?

Any time. Any place. Any issue.

Mediations can even happen on the eve of the court date—and often do. The harsh realities of a courtroom trial can drive some participants to choose mediation at the eleventh hour.

Studies show, however, that an early intervention—a quick detour into mediation—produces better results. It may be that the parties are more flexible before pride—or the bills from their lawyers—commits them to a hard-and-fast position.

Keep in mind that mediation—as an alternative to the courtroom—can be suggested by either party at any stage of the dispute and judges are increasingly willing to accommodate mediation requests. If the other party agrees, you're miles ahead.

Mediation holds out the possibility of getting the dispute settled so you can get on with your life—without waiting on the court docket for a trial date.

Sometimes the judge will either suggest or order mediation. Unfortunately, not all judges hold the same beliefs about mediation; some will use the word "mediation" while in their minds, they are really thinking "settlement conference."

There is not much to be gained from trying to out-talk a judge, and don't ever, EVER, interrupt a judge—a respectful *"Yes, your Honor"* goes a long way—but if you have a good opportunity, ask the judge for her/his definition of mediation and remember, it isn't mediation if you are going to be "required" to agree or if you do not have full right to self-determination.

Frequently, mediations take place without attorneys. However, if the stakes are high, parties may be more comfortable having an attorney at hand or available to help them understand the consequences of making or accepting any offers, or waiving any rights. Lawyers who attend a mediation session literally take a back seat; their role is to advise, not to advocate. While there may be advocacy in mediation from time to time, there is a great deal of difference between person-to-person persuasion and legal power.

All parties have an opportunity to say things during a mediation that would never be heard in court. Mediation allows people to reveal their human side.

A widespread belief of legal lore leads people to sometimes equate an apology to an admission of guilt. In the informal atmosphere of a mediation, people can be more open and can honestly express their understanding and concern over another person's problems or circumstances. In the courtroom, lawyers have learned to fear a misconstrued apology.

It takes a lot to astonish a mediator. With but a few cases under their belts, most mediators have seen the best and the worst in people. But almost every mediator with a few years of experience can share a story during professional workshops—all identifying characteristics removed, of course—of how a mediation session turned on a simple apology.

Often the mediator had been nearing the bottom of her/his list of strategies when one party, or both, unexpectedly offered an apology. Mediators quote one of the participants as saying something like: *"All I ever really wanted was an apology,"* or *"if I had ever heard 'I'm sorry,' things would never have gotten this far."*

Apologizing, or forgiving, doesn't mean the monetary or property issues are going to go away, but suddenly seeing each other as ordinary, decent human beings can make other issues easier to resolve.

Suppose there is no agreement, and the case still

goes to trial? If nothing else, rest assured that everyone involved will have learned a very powerful lesson from the opportunities not taken to settle the matter before the judge or jury decides the matter for them.

Mediation remains a very effective means to resolve a dispute. Next time you feel like seeking retribution, consider first the expenses and aggravations of filing—and seeing to completion—a lawsuit.

Mediation is not an instant cure-all for everything. Sometimes a session will end—abruptly—with no agreement but with disgruntled participants. After a couple of days of calm reflection, however, parties can see more clearly and often seek a return to mediation because they are now more willing to consider an offer they earlier rejected.

Revenge is sweet, but sweeter yet for the long-haul is saving hundreds (if not thousands) of dollars in legal costs and expenses, restoring good relationships (or if you never expect to see the other party again, at least parting on better terms), and letting you keep hours (days, weeks, months … years) of your own time.

You've got better things to do than permitting a rancorous conflict to occupy all of your waking hours—and some of the sleeping ones too! Mediation is almost always a better first step than litigation.

SCHOOL YARD GAMES
(Mediation and Our Kids)

Chapter Seven

Your kid comes home from school with a bruised cheek, the result of an altercation with a classmate.

You don't want your child to go back to school the next day and start a fight, but you think it only fair that s/he have the opportunity to stand up for her/himself.

The next week your child and the offender are co-captains of the soccer team.

SCHOOL YARD GAMES

What the blank is going on?

"Peer" is the word you will hear to describe mediation programs which have been established in many schools.

A successful peer mediation program requires a committed adult as a leader, backed by strong support from the principal and school district administrative personnel. The mediation sessions are actually conducted by trained students serving as mediators with oversight or supervision as needed.

School mediation programs are functioning at all age levels.

Pre-school or kindergarten children may be asked to come to sit together at a "peace" table following a confrontation. University students who find themselves involved in a housing dispute may have the option of taking their problems to a campus mediation service.

At any grade level, students in conflict may be able to discuss their issues with the assistance of peer mediators, classmates who have been trained to listen without taking sides.

The availability of a peer mediation program helps children learn "people skills" that allow them to interact with other individuals in a non-threatening manner.

Rather than trying to determine fault—who was right or who was wrong—peer mediators treat the conflict as the "problem" and give the participants (make that combatants in some cases) the opportunity to work together as partners to find a solution.

Both—or all—parties to the conflict will be given equal time to explore what happened. All parties will be listened to with equal attention. Each participant will be encouraged to propose options that can lead to a resolution.

The pattern for reaching resolutions in peer mediation is similar to adult mediation. The first step—if the process is truly mediation—is to confirm that the children agree that they are willing to participate.

The fall-back alternative for any student not willing to participate might be the traditional route: a *"trip to the principal's office."*

Traditional disciplinary methods usually do not distinguish between incidents which are the result of breaking the rules and those which are interpersonal conflicts. Punishments—negative reinforcements—are applied equally for both types of unacceptable behavior.

The heart of the mediation process is asking each student to relate their version of the quarrel. The student mediator should remain calm and neutral. Often, the sessions may include one or more "observers" who are part of the training process.

When the student mediator feels that all parties have been given all the space they need to air their grievances, s/he may ask each party to repeat what they think the other party has said; the students in conflict don't necessarily have to agree with the other party, but they are asked to demonstrate that they understand their opponent's position.

After the conflict has been isolated, parties are asked to brainstorm ideas for resolution. Here's where an observer can help by writing the suggestions on a chalk-board, a flip-chart, or maybe simply a piece of paper.

It's sometimes hard even for adult mediators to keep from rushing the process and be too eager to reach a resolution too soon. Ideally, mediation should proceed at a deliberative pace.

Mediation works for adults because people are more likely to comply with an agreement they have helped to create than with an order issued by a judge. Mediation works for kids, too, and for the same reasons—having a chance to work out mutual resolutions produces a better outcome than enduring a punishment administered by a teacher or a principal.

The first organized school mediation programs date from the 1960's. Many schools across the country have successfully established long-running programs. Students who have several years of experience may be asked to demonstrate conflict resolution and mediation training in other schools.

There are many schools in which there is no peer mediation conflict resolution program. Schools in which a principal or a teacher are trying to get a peer mediation program started need all the help they can get.

If a new program is underway at your child's school, the sponsors will welcome your interest and your support. Properly practiced mediation almost never hurts—and it might help.

GETTING YOUR SHARE
(Probate Mediation)

Chapter Eight

There's a guy in northern Alabama probably still driving around with a stuffed buffalo head in the trunk of his old car.

He rarely opens the trunk because whenever that glass-eyed buffalo looks back at him, he gets angry all over again.

He first met that particular buffalo when an older

Getting Your Share

cousin took him on a wild, wandering trip through North Dakota and the West.

They found the stuffed buffalo head at a cluttered roadside gasoline station somewhere in Montana and bought it for three dollars from an overworked clerk who was glad to see it go. By the time they got back to Alabama, they had concocted several different variations of how the unfortunate animal had fallen into their hands. Some of the stories ribald and all of them colorful—putting the rambling cousins in the best of light. They hung the head on the wall of the older cousin's wood-working shop.

They never admitted the truth. After several years of mutually-instigated recitations, after stories of the cousins' buffalo hunting glory had become a local legend, the older cousin took his part of the secret to his grave. And the surviving cousin thought the buffalo head rightfully belonged to him.

Not so.

Following several unsuccessful efforts to claim the buffalo head from his cousin's grown children, he learned that the cousin's worldly goods would be disposed of through an estate sale.

He cashed his weekly paycheck on the morning of the sale, and had lots of money, but he was thinking in terms of three dollars.

Several hours later he left the sale, both poorer and richer. Richer in that he now owned the buffalo head he so long had prized but poorer by leaving a goodly sum of money in the cash box of the sales clerk. When he put the buffalo head in the trunk of his car, he was the angriest he had ever been.

He left his purchase in the car for as long as we know, which kept it out of sight, but every time he had to open the trunk, all his anger came flooding back.

Of all the yarns spun by the cousins, the ending was an unhappy tale. Unfortunately, not a bit uncommon, which is what can make going through probate an unpleasant experience for many people.

Has anyone ever died and left behind a perfectly-executable set of instructions? Unwilling to contemplate their own departure, most people fail to leave clear directions about their wishes. Others are so painstakingly thorough that their executors may spend a year trying to figure out which Red Willow gravy boat with an almost-matching ladle goes to which great-niece or ex-neighbor's granddaughter-in-law, or which great nephew or third cousin (twice removed) will receive the First Edition Monopoly Game with all playing pieces intact.

The only person who can indulge in hopes of receiving the entire estate of a deceased person is an only child, who is also a sole survivor. Everyone else must hold their breath until the will is read, or if there is no will, wait for the decisions of a probate judge. And even wills give rise to contests and fights and arguments of all nature.

Whether it's money, or property, or sentimental mementos, emotions are keenly felt. People remember for the rest of their lives what they failed to get.

It's almost certain that not everyone is going to get everything they want from the deceased person's estate. **Fortunately, no one wants to be described as greedy, and even the most selfish of relatives find it hard to argue against the concept of fairness.**

Adhering to the wishes of the departed is complicated enough but trying to do that while dealing with the living is even more complicated. Numerous systems have been devised and utilized to solve such difficulties, such as having the inheritors take turns in choosing who gets what. Sometimes it helps to get the advice of professional appraisers. Some families draw lots. Others fight or stew.

Unless the deceased has left a very small estate, and the few inheritors are very congenial, the whole process might be more easily completed with the services of a neutral third-party.

Some states in which court administrators have observed the beneficial uses of mediation in juvenile programs, small claims, and post-divorce matters have moved forward to initiate probate mediation. Such programs are relatively new and exist in only a handful of states.

No one wants to anticipate someone's death, but it's always better to be prepared in advance. If you think that you may soon be a recipient of an elderly relative's estate, make a few discreet inquiries about the availability of mediation programs.

If there is no probate mediation program currently in place, there is nothing that prevents you from talking to a private mediator.

When the time comes and you and the other inheritors are dividing an estate—hopefully with the help of a mediator—you still won't get everything you want, you may not wind up with the stuffed buffalo head, but everyone involved can emerge with the feeling that the distribution has been fair.

WHO INVENTED MEDIATION?
(Does it Matter?)

Chapter Nine

Some mediators are willing to claim that mediators invented mediation, which is laughable, because twenty-five years ago most people who were mediating didn't even know what to call themselves.

Some lawyers wish they had invented mediation and are working hard to bring mediation into a strictly legal realm. They would patent it, given half a chance!

Who Invented Mediation?

The truth is mediation has been with us forever. It doesn't matter who invented mediation. And, you should know, no one has the exclusive right to market one form of mediation over any other. What matters is putting mediation to use.

Much of the popularity—and increased availability—of mediation can be traced to the dedication and persistence of faith communities. The longest-running mediation programs were started and sustained by individuals whose motivation has been to fulfill personal lifechoices, not to recruit new converts to their religion.

Who invented conciliation, early neutral evaluation, settlement conferences, arbitration (binding and non-binding), family circle conferencing, etc., and some of the other alternative dispute resolution models? It would take several books to trace the history of these various forms of dispute resolution.

People who do not know the differences conveniently lump many of them all together and call them "mediation." The difference between mediation and these alternative forms of dispute resolution is easy to spot.

It's not that hard:

Self-Determination

Self-Determination

Self-Determination

And that difference is very important. In fact, understanding, using and applying self-determination is the single most important part of mediation.

On the internet, you can find dozens of definitions of mediation, no two alike.

From the website of the Arkansas Alternative Dispute Resolution Commission:

> *Mediation is a non-adversarial process in which the objective is the encouragement and facilitation of a mutually acceptable agreement based on the parties self-determined needs, interests and values.*

The Wyoming Mediation Guide describes mediation as follows:

> *Agreements reached in mediation are more likely to be followed, as opposed to a court order or arbitrators' decision, because the individuals are the decision makers.*

The Federal Mediation and Conciliation Service guidelines include:

> *Mediation is a voluntary process, and the mediator has no authority to compel disputing parties to accept contract terms.*

Mediation Rule Number One in the state of Minnesota is:

> *A mediator shall recognize that mediation is based on the principle of self-determination by the parties. It requires that the mediation process rely upon the ability of the parties to reach a voluntary, un-coerced agreement. The primary responsibility for the resolution of a dispute and the shaping of a settlement agreement rests with the parties. A mediator shall not require a party to stay in the mediation against the party's will.*

Who Invented Mediation?

While the exact definition of mediation may not be clear, it is clear is that mediation puts you—and your opponent—equally in the driver's seat.

> **ROADMAP—**
>
> The parties have joint control of where the mediation is going. If either one of you is being steered or pressured in a direction where you do not want to go, the parties have lost control, and the process is no longer mediation—whatever else it might be.

If you are looking for an easy test to figure out if what is being done is a mediation, ask the simple question: "Am I required to agree to any of this?" Anytime the answer is that you are required to agree to something, it is no longer mediation and you may want to think about stopping.

Another simple test to help figure out whether mediation is being practiced, is whether the mediator is giving you "advice." Let's say you have been participating in mediation and your "mediator" starts telling you, *"Hey, Dude, if you don't accept this offer that the other party has made to you, the judge will throw your case out of court."* Or, you might hear, perhaps in caucus, *"Your evidence won't hold up in court. What the other party is offering you is a lot more than you'll ever get from the judge. You better take it."*

If the "mediator" begins giving this sort of advice—or any advice for that matter—it's probably time for you to ask her/him where s/he got her/his training in "settlement conferences" or "early neutral evaluation." These other forms of alternative dispute resolution can be very useful, but should never be confused with mediation. It is a very subtle nuance to mediation but mediation does not depend on whether one or the other of the parties will have the better case in court or can get more money or a better deal some other way.

The parties, by creating their own self-shaped agreement to resolve their dispute, are free to value (and evaluate) what is important to them without guessing how other people might view the situation. Successful mediation often depends upon the parties' willingness to consider possible resolutions to their differences—some of which may be found well beyond the limits of courtroom-bound law.

The "unauthorized practice of law" means giving legal advice without a license. Mediators shudder at the mention of the phrase. As a participant in mediation, you should shudder, too, if it appears that the mediator is giving legal advice.

Your decisions in mediation should be based on what you are willing to do, balanced against what the other party is willing to do. The Agreement to Mediate form that you probably signed at the beginning most likely had some warning that the mediator cannot act as an attorney and under no circumstances will be giving legal advice during the mediation.

The expectation that no legal advice should be given in a mediation session makes it difficult for some lawyers to function as mediators. Lawyers sometimes find it hard to step away from their

Who Invented Mediation?

customary role as advocates—that is why some lawyers make better judges than others. Not everyone can be neutral.

And, if the mediator is not a lawyer, can you (or should you) mediate without a lawyer? That's your decision. Many lawyers will tell you "No way!" but remember: you—and the other party—are the ones in charge—not the lawyers. Often, the nature of the conflict will help you determine whether or not you will want the advice of a lawyer either during or after mediation. Ask yourself what is at stake. Does your dispute involve the future of your children? Will any decision that is reached involve a large sum of money?

You might ask yourself what you really want for the outcome. Are you willing to be satisfied with a judicial decision that would award custody, money, or property to you? Or would you like for one of the results of mediation to be a lessening of hostility and an improvement of whatever relationship may continue into the future?

A judge can award custody, or can order the other party to give you money or property. A judge can order someone to avoid all contact with you. **But there is no way any judge can ever order anyone to change the way they feel about you.**

Mediators are happy to have lawyers present during the mediation, but they expect the lawyers to take a back-row seat, available to provide legal advice, but not to advocate. Mediators are equally happy to mediate without lawyers in attendance, which would probably save you some money anyway. Most lawyers can be available at the other end of a cell-phone when you need them—if you need them.

In many circumstances, mediators may suggest that the parties have their attorneys review any proposed agreement before they actually sign the document. Given these instructions, the parties are free to decide for themselves whether to ask a lawyer to look at the document.

Exceptions can occur in those states which by law prohibit litigants from bringing an attorney to represent them in small claims court cases. Since the parties in those states represent themselves, attorneys are not readily available for consultation.

Ironic, isn't it, that a judge can order you to participate in a procedure that is based on self-determination? Long experience has shown judges that in a majority of cases people who have mutually created their own agreements are far happier with the outcomes than they are with boiler-plate decisions.

Remember, if the "mediator" starts telling you what will happen if your case goes before a judge, or strongly pushing for a decision that the "mediator" believes is in your best interests, it is no longer mediation. In those cases, the "mediator" is more interested in getting a settlement than in helping the parties create their own resolution. Your decision to resolve your dispute should not be based upon pressure or advice from your mediator.

You have many authority figures in your life—a mediator should not be one of them.

WHY NOT YOU?
(Exploring Mediation and You)

Chapter Ten

Have you read most of the book? Except for maybe that long Nuts and Bolts second chapter you can always go back to read?

Mediation doesn't seem all that scary, anymore, does it? Now that you understand the process, you have the tools you need to look out for your interests and to build an agreement that will put an end to your dispute.

Along the way, you may have become more aware of how often people use informal mediation—maybe not by that name—to resolve issues of everyday life.

Bargaining—bartering, swapping, trading, exchanging—is what we do all the time. We'd sure like to buy that new computer which costs a LOT of money. The merchant sees us wavering and knows that s/he will have to offer more options or enhancements to finalize the sale. It is a process of considering alternatives and trade-offs.

Mediation is simply a more organized way of discussing the trade-offs.

Mediation can be applied to problems both large and small—public or private.

Maybe you really want to take your kids out-of-state during the winter school break, because your mother gets depressed if she can't see her grandchildren over the holidays, while your ex-spouse gets a bigger kick out of taking the kids to the beach or the mountains or the amusement parks in the summertime. Those are options that may be worked out through mediation.

We often read in the newspapers or hear television announcers talk about mediators being sent around the globe. We come to view mediation as an open, public process. When you learn that the President is sending the Secretary of State on a very visible trip to mediate with two warring groups, the high-profile emissary will mediate. S/he will also negotiate, explain, persuade, dissuade, convince, offer options, cajole, entreat, implore, apply pressure, and emphasize positions. In fact, the "mediator" will be engaged in diplomacy of the highest level. Mediation will be only one of many strategic concepts that might be employed, although it is doubtful that there will be any thumb-wrestling involved.

By this time, you may begin to suspect that sub-groupings of mediation styles and concepts have evolved within mediation.

Every mediator has her/his own distinctive style, or mixture of styles, modes of conducting mediations which, in her/his experience, have most consistently produced satisfactory, enduring results for all parties.

All competent, knowledgeable mediators understand the three major types of mediation, can give you a thumbnail description of each, and will be happy to tell you whether they prefer evaluative, transformative, or facilitative mediation.

As the name suggests, during an evaluative mediation, the mediator helps the parties evaluate their positions, with some consideration as to what the outcome might be if the dispute were to be taken into the courtroom.

The mediator has to maintain a lot of self-control to keep an evaluative mediation session within the framework of pure mediation. It is very difficult for some mediators to encourage parties to take a long, hard look at the reality of their situation without arriving at—and being tempted to give a voice to—the mediator's personal opinion about the merits of either party's situation. Remember that in mediation, the actual or even probable legal outcome does not necessarily hold the answer for the parties' resolution.

If the mediator ventures an opinion about how the dispute might be handled by a judge or jury, s/he is veering dangerously close to giving legal advice. If attorneys are present, and give legal advice to parties, the procedure is really mediation in name only and should more properly be called a settlement conference or early neutral evaluation.

Transformative mediation is a time-honored concept about how best to deal with conflict that has gained wider recognition in the past dozen or so years.

In desperation, following several horrifying episodes—some involving multiple fatalities—at postal worksites, authorities looked toward the mediation community for answers about how to stop the violence.

Several extensive pilot programs led postal authorities to conclude that a transformative style of mediation produced useful results.

Transformative mediation differs from traditional models by giving the parties control not only for the outcome but for the process as well. Aside from the scheduled time and location of mediation, all of the other details about how the mediation will proceed are decisions to be made mutually by the parties and not the mediator.

In facilitative mediation, the mediator controls the process. The mediator jump-starts the discussions by setting out some ground rules and being more direct about how the session will be conducted.

As might be expected, a facilitative mediation session will probably conclude in a shorter time.

WHY NOT YOU?

Although in all mediations it is best that the suggestions for potential resolutions come from the parties, a facilitative mediator is more likely to offer—perhaps to move beyond an impasse—additional options that the parties have not previously introduced.

An evaluative mediator might make a suggestion saying *"You should ...."* A facilitative mediator would ask *"Have you ever considered thinking about ...."*

Transformative mediators, particularly if they are conducting a postal work-site mediation, will take great pains to not deviate from transformative guidelines. In other situations, both facilitative and transformative mediators may use concepts taken from both styles.

The differences, having been developed through the work of innumerable mediators in uncounted disputes, are not insignificant but are not something you need to understand for your first mediation.

After you have gone through the mediation process as a participant, after you have learned that mediation can be fair to all parties, how the process allows people to express their emotions, even anger, and then gain control over it, how any and all options can be given equal consideration, and how no agreement is final until all of the parties freely and voluntarily agree, there is one more step you can take. You can become part of the process. You might consider becoming a mediator yourself.

The mediation field is blessed with the contributions of people from all walks of life. Mediation is bigger than the legal realm. Mediation encompasses more than the literal letter of the law. Mediation gives people the power to reach agreements to do things by voluntary and mutual consent that could never be ordered by a court.

You don't need any kind of specialized education to be a mediator. What you do need is the vision and ability to see that there can be many ways to resolve a dispute. When that idea has taken up permanent residence in your mind, it's time for you to share your convictions.

There is a place for you in the mediation world. Maybe you would never want to be more deeply involved than volunteering in a community center or small claims court. Maybe you want to explore mediation as a full-time career. It's a challenge to find a niche, but very rewarding—sometimes even monetarily—for those who have found the opportunities to prove their worth.

You could explore the possibilities by getting some mediation training. Basic courses can be done in a week, or maybe spread over two or three weekends. If most of what you learn consists of ideas that already make a lot of sense to you, you've come to the right place.

One of the greatest things that happens during mediation training is the chance to rub elbows, enjoy tea and chocolate chip cookies (or broccoli and diet cheese dip) and swap "peace stories" with people who are thinking along the same lines as you may be.

Typical course offerings might include:

Accommodating Disability in Mediation
Beyond the Basic Parenting Plan

> *Case Management in Difficult Divorces*
> *Civil Mediation Training*
> *Domestic Relations Mediation Training*
> *Parent/Adolescent Mediation Training*
> *Juvenile Dependence Mediation*

There are also courses in:

> *Mediation in the Workplace*
> *Negotiating Win/Win Solutions*
> *Principles of Core Mediation*
> *Establishing Peer Mediation*
> *Mediating In Probate Court*
> *Principles of Restorative Justice*
> *Questioning and Listening Wisdom for Mediators*
> *Trying To Do It Right: Mediation Ethics*
> *The Use of Mediation Principles in Collaborative Law*
> *Victim Offender Mediator Training ...*

And more! Whew!

Many colleges also offer courses in conflict resolution, or alternative dispute resolution. A number of universities offer postgraduate degrees in conflict resolution. Several of them involve online, distance-learning programs that require a minimum of on-campus time. There are even a few law schools where lawyer-mediators can earn an LL.M. degree.

The beauty of mediation is that you can enter the field at any point, and you can continue to pursue educational goals at your own speed. The practice of mediation is richly enhanced by the huge range of life experiences that mediators bring to the mediation session.

So, after all is said and done, the next time your neighbor's hound-dog wakes you up at 2:30 in the morning, don't start looking for your shotgun. Instead, take out the phonebook and look for the telephone number of your community mediation center.

There's no listing?

Well, someone needs to help get one started.

Why not you?

GUIDEPOSTS
(Making Mediation Work for You)

Chapter Eleven

This chapter is last on purpose. People regularly ask: "What is the BEST strategy for getting what I want in mediation?"

And this book wouldn't be complete without an answer.

But the "best" answer won't satisfy everyone.

Based upon years of mediation and gazillions of mediation conversations, the best strategy is understanding and putting to use the power of Self-Determination.

Some people seem to think that there are secret tricks and traps and psychological ploys and downright cheating that can be used in mediation. Perhaps their experience with people—call it cynicism!—makes them reason that there must be. And, maybe there are. But all of them can be defeated by Self-Determination.

Self-Determination, when used, is like veto power. Everyone is free to decide not to agree. It won't matter how many clever tricks or traps or strategies one side might try on the other. Self-Determination means that no party can be forced or required to agree to anything they do not want to.

Mediation, if we are willing to put it to work for us, clearly marks humans as different from less sentient beings:

— the fact that we are capable of engaging in mediation efforts to resolve disputes,
— replacing force or even violence with communication, civility and conversation,
— working toward a free and voluntary resolution of differences.

We can choose to be different from animals.

Or, as Bing Crosby once sang: "Would you rather be a mule?"

Of course it would have been easier (and much faster for you) to just skip ahead to this little mediation outline. Did you? Don't forget that the rest of the book contains all sorts of useful information. Go back and read through Chapter Two on Nuts and Bolts. Read through the chapters on specific mediation situations. You will find helpful ideas in most of the chapters. Things that you might take with you for later use.

GUIDE-POSTS
(NOT QUITE RULES!)
FOR MEDIATION SURVIVAL

2.   **SELF-DETERMINATION**—you have power and control in mediation.

PREPARING FOR MEDIATION

3.   Before going to the mediation, think about what outcomes are important to you—that is: what do you want or expect from mediation? Make a list.

4.   Also, try to think about what may be important to the other side. Try to see the other side's point of view. Make a list.

5.   Thinking about the two lists, what are the likely disagreements? What are the likely agreements? What are the areas where you can work toward a resolution? Make a list.

6.   Jot down a couple of suggestions for what you think it would take to solve the problem being mediated—just don't get too committed to any one idea (remember that the other side is probably doing the same thing). You can't force the other side to

agree to what you want anymore than they could force you to agree with what they might want. Mediation requires voluntary agreement.

AT THE MEDIATION

7. At the mediation, is the mediator someone you can work with? Do you feel the mediator is capable? Qualified?

8. Are there any conflicts of interest that need to be discussed?

9. How much will the mediation cost? And, who is going to pay how much? When?

10. Remember that the mediator is not "in charge" of your mediation, you are. One way of looking at it is asking yourself if you think this mediator will be fair to the parties?

11. Make sure you understand confidentiality requirements and expectations.

12. Take time to calmly read the "agreement to mediate." Ask the mediator to explain anything you do not understand. Make sure you understand what you and the other party(ies) are committing to before signing.

13. Do you feel comfortable in the mediation setting? Again, speak up for yourself if you don't.

14. Ask questions! Get comfortable or change! If you can't change, think about what might be done to help make you comfortable.

MEDIATE

15. Remember that, while you control your power to agree and disagree—**SELF-DETERMINATION!**— you need to hear what the other side is saying.

16. Be a good listener. Consider what the other side has to say. Try to understand the circumstances that makes them take the position that they are taking. Be open and flexible to alternative resolutions. Try to see what is possible, what is practical. What would work things out?

17. There are very few areas in life where being polite and courteous to others will pay more dividends.

18. When it is your turn, describe what you would like to see done, be prepared to say why, to describe what is important to you. Be courteous, be reasonable.

19. Keep emotions under control.

20. Don't be afraid to ask to take a break if that will help.

21. Mediation is a conversation looking for an agreement. It can be straight-forward and cut-and-dried but more often it will have stops and starts and twists and turns along the way. Remain open. Stay flexible. Be courteous.

22. Remember that there may be several "rounds" to the mediation conversation. There may even be caucus sessions, separating the parties into different rooms for private talks. Later meetings may be scheduled.

REACHING RESOLUTION

23. Mediation is not about whose "facts" are correct.

24. Mediation is not about what "the law" or the judge says is correct, who can hire the better lawyer, or who might win in court.

25. The power and strength of mediation—and it is very subtle—is that **SELF-DETERMINATION** gives the parties the power to reach any resolution they can voluntarily agree to without regard to facts, the law, testimony, evidence, the government or any other outside influence. This is the simplicity and beauty of **SELF-DETERMINATION**: the parties can shape a resolution that fits them on the issues that are important to them. If they can reach a voluntary agreement, they are not bound to courtroom law and can shape their mediation resolution to any legal agreement that the parties are free to enter into.

26. The only real limitation on mediation resolution is that the parties cannot agree to do illegal acts. Sometimes courts will want to review—or even approve—mediation agreements. For the most part, they are doing that to protect the powerless from the over-powering. That is why the weak are given total right to **SELF-DETERMINATION**. It protects them—when they are willing to protect themselves.

27. If the parties reach agreement, write it down as clearly as possible. You might have the mediator or someone else be the person who writes the agreement. It is best, when possible, to write things down at the mediation session. You would be surprised how quickly memory changes.

28. <u>Before</u> signing the concluding document, the "mediation agreement," make certain that you understand everything you and the other party(ies) are committing to. Ask questions about anything you do not understand. You may want to have your lawyer or other independent advisor review the proposed "mediation agreement." In most cases, the written "mediation agreement" will be a binding contract once it has been signed.

29. Remember: mediation's right and power of **SELF-DETERMINATION** means that none of the parties can be forced or required to agree to anything. If, and only if, the proposed "mediation agreement" is something that will solve the mediation issues and is an agreement that you are willing to voluntarily enter into and you are willing and able to live by its terms, requirements and conditions, enter into the agreement.

30. Under all other conditions or possibilities, continue the mediation conversation looking for resolution. Sometimes, but rarely, the only agreement the parties can reach is that they cannot agree.

RULE NUMBER ONE

1. **YOU WILL SURVIVE**—if you understand and use your power and right of **SELF-DETERMINATION!**

GOOD LUCK. I WISH YOU THE BEST—IN PEACE.

Go Forth And Mediate!

ACKNOWLEDGEMENTS

To everyone who has shared my journey:

You have all contributed to my growth as a mediator in ways too numerous to measure. It is utterly impossible to acknowledge everyone by name.

In the beginning steps of my journey, I am grateful to have received a "Recognition of Outstanding Voluntary Service," from the Dispute Resolution Services, signed by Karl Johnson and Helen Wahl of Kansas Legal Services.

Receiving that honor confirmed to me that I was on the right path.

When I began that journey in 1994, I had the great, good fortune to be associated with the courtroom of Magistrate Judge Michael H. Farley, in my opinion, absolutely the best Small Claims judge in the entire United States. My luck continued by working next with the second (but only chronologically) best Small Claims judge in the country, Magistrate Judge Linda Trigg.

I treasure (and am not sure I have truly earned) the Acorn Award ... 'For Planting the Seeds of Professionalism, Networking, and Education that have Grown into the Heartland Mediators Association and for Her Role in Cultivating These Values as a Member.'

Parvis E Glandibus Quercus.

I'm still nourishing my little seedling oak tree.

I happily accepted the Liberty Bell Award from the Johnson County Bar Association in 2003, "In Grateful Appreciation for Outstanding Community Service by Encouraging a Greater Respect for Law and the Courts," because I felt I was accepting the honor and recognition on behalf of the volunteer mediators and mediation students who have been associated with the Small Claims Mediation Program from its inception.

For those volunteer mediators and students I never thanked before, let me do so now. Your inspiration to me, and to your colleagues, has never been forgotten.

To those of you who knew I was working on a book about mediation, this is probably not what you expected.

This book is not really for you, it's for the people who need you.

It's for people who have never talked to a mediator, people who do not understand mediation, people who are afraid of mediation, and people who think that mediation is some kind of mysterious process.

Mediators have a gift for these people—as a mediator, you can give them the gift of realizing that often the power to solve many of the conflicts in their lives can lie in their own hands.

Peg Nichols
Olathe, Kansas
February, 2006

Mediation Survivor's Handbook

THE ART OF THE BOOK

The text in this book is set in Imperial 11 pt.

Cover text includes Impact and Ninja Naruto.

Ninja Naruto is designed by sk89q. Derivative typeface © 2004 The Risen Realm (http://www.therisenrealm.com) and Keiichi Anime Forever (http://anime.therisenrealm.com). Original type © Kishimoto Masashi, Shueisha, TV Tokyo. All Rights Reserved.

Cover designed by Britt Nichols.

Design Consulting by Jane Rogers
Typesetting and layout by Rex Rogers.

Printed by Central Plains Book Manufacturing
Winfield, Kansas

NOTES

NOTES

NOTES

NOTES

NOTES

NOTES

NOTES

HOW TO ORDER

Additional copies and current editions may be obtained from the publisher either on-line at *http://www.mediationsurvivorshandbook.com* or from:

WeirBox Press
P.O. Box 382
Olathe, Kansas,
United States
66051-0382

HOW TO PARTICIPATE

Please also visit *http://mediationbychoice.blogspot.com* to participate in an on-going mediation conversation.

HOW TO CONTACT

Your author may be contacted at
mediationsurvival@att.net